"This is a highly relevant book... keeping up with the development of artificial intelligence technology to stay relevant in the digital era and to be able to effectively integrate AI into work processes, adding value to your personal and professional performance." — **YULIIA SUKHOVERKHA**

"I love it!" — **GUNTA M.**

"A cracking guide for anyone curious about AI but put off by the usual technobabble. Melissa has this brilliant knack for stripping down complex concepts, like machine learning and neural networks, into something even a layperson could wrap their head around. It's rich with practical examples that ground the theory and hands-on exercises that genuinely bridge the gap between reading and actually using AI. She doesn't shy away from the tough stuff either, digging into ethical concerns and highlighting AI's current limits without sugar-coating." — **PAUL BYRNE**

"A must-read for anyone curious about AI." — **KARLYGASH IMANBAYEVA**

"*Essentials of AI for Beginners* is a thoroughly accessible and engaging book for all readers. Demystifying AI is not an easy task, and this manages to be informative, interactive, and keeps you engaged throughout. The use of interactive exercises is particularly helpful to understand (and apply!) complex ideas to practical learning." — **MEL K.**

"A fantastic read for beginners like me!" — **NICOLE VICENTIC**

"I found the suggested tools really useful! What would take me hours to write now takes me minutes. That's a WIN in my book." — **MELISSA LEITHWOOD**

PRAISE FOR ESSENTIALS OF AI FOR BEGINNERS

"How can making a tomato and cheese sandwich, baking a cake, tying my shoes, or deciding whether to go outside to garden teach me about AI? That's how Peneycad does it. She creates analogies, offers many practical examples, and simplifies the topic. This book was a pleasure to read. It was fast-paced yet comprehensive." — **EDWARD WEDLER**

"Extremely informative book." — **GREG EDMONDSON**

"This is a strongly substantive book, covering everything from AI fundamentals and practical applications to hands-on technical learning emphasizing coding and the use of generative AI tools. From ethics and governance to creativity, lifelong learning, and AI careers, this book has it all. Essentials? For beginners? Yes, to both!" — **DAVID REYNOLDS**

"*Essentials of AI for Beginners* is a fantastic guide for anyone curious about AI. Melissa makes complex topics feel accessible and engaging, and her real-world examples bring AI to life in a way that feels immediately relevant. Whether you're looking to enhance your career or just want to understand the technology shaping our world, this book is the perfect starting point." — **CHRISTIAN BROWNE**

"This is just the book I've been looking for!" — **SEDEF YAVUZ NOYAN**

"Melissa has a true gift. She writes about such an intricate topic with utmost clarity and makes learning enjoyable. I appreciate everything Melissa is doing in the field of AI. I look forward to her future titles." — **LORRAINE STEVENSON**

"You can't begin to understand how much this has helped me as a student going into the IT world, especially with the section on career pathways." — **ZOE K.**

"A must-have book in anyone's library." — **BARB W.**

"This book stands out with very well-curated content that goes beyond the basics, offering an in-depth yet accessible exploration I have not found in other resources. The explanations are thorough without overwhelming beginners, making it perfect for anyone seeking a comprehensive, approachable guide. Highly recommended!" — **NEGIN FICZKOWSKI**

"Masterfully captures the essentials of AI. The future is exciting, and this book is a fantastic introduction to this significant topic!" — **DAMIAN ALI**

"This is the AI book you want." — **BRIAN C.**

"With AI fast becoming an integral part of our everyday lives and work lives, I've been feeling off-kilter about how to tackle this subject. So [*Essentials of AI for Beginners*] came at just the right moment! I love the clarity. This book encompasses many aspects of the subject, but I have not once felt overwhelmed! Bravo!" — **ALKISTIS BESTEL**

"An empowering resource." — **RITA ASSI NJWENG**

"I recently completed an AI course, and I honestly think this book should have been a mandatory reading." — **COLLETTE DESCHENES**

"A must-read for anyone looking to understand AI without a technical background...It's informative, engaging, and empowering." — **RADMILLO BODIROGA**

ESSENTIALS OF AI FOR BEGINNERS

UNLOCK THE POWER OF MACHINE LEARNING, GENERATIVE AI & CHATGPT TO ADVANCE YOUR CAREER, BOOST CREATIVITY & KEEP PACE WITH MODERN INNOVATIONS EVEN IF YOU'RE NOT TECH-SAVVY

MELISSA PENEYCAD

© **Copyright Melissa Peneycad 2024 - All rights reserved. Published by Clover Lane Publishing.**

No part of this book may be reproduced, duplicated, or transmitted in any form or by any means without prior written permission from the author or publisher.

The author and publisher disclaim any responsibility or liability for any direct or indirect damages or loss resulting from using the information in this book. Readers assume full responsibility for their own actions and results.

Legal Notice:

This book is protected by copyright law. It is for personal use only and may not be altered, distributed, sold, quoted, or paraphrased without the written consent of the author or publisher.

Disclaimer Notice:

The information in this book is provided for educational and informational purposes only. While all efforts have been made to ensure accuracy and completeness, no warranties or guarantees of any kind are expressed or implied. The author is not providing legal, financial, medical, or professional advice. Readers are advised to consult with a licensed professional before implementing any techniques or advice in this book.

By using this book, readers agree that the author and publisher are not liable for any direct or indirect losses resulting from errors, omissions, or inaccuracies in the content.

CONTENTS

Introduction	xi
1. AI FUNDAMENTALS	**1**
Artificial Intelligence Explained	2
Teaching Machines to Learn	6
Mimicking The Human Brain	7
Going Deeper with AI	11
AI's Trio: ML, NN, and DL	11
The AI Spectrum: Narrow to Super AI	13
Simple Algorithms to Advanced Systems	14
Chapter 1 Self-Assessment	16
2. PRACTICAL APPLICATIONS OF AI	**17**
Healthcare Innovations and Impacts	18
Shaping Modern Banking	20
Enhancing Customer Experience in Retail and E-Commerce	22
Transforming the Entertainment Industry	24
Personalizing Learning and Accelerating Research	26
Improving Workplace Efficiency and Collaboration	28
Cofounder to Intern: AI and Entrepreneurship	30
Protecting the Public with AI	33
Applying AI Skills in Your Current Job	35
Everyday AI	37
Chapter 2 Self-Assessment	38
3. HANDS-ON EXPLORATION OF AI	**39**
Getting Started with AI Tools	39
Python Basics	42
Hands-on Activities using Python	44
The Importance of Version Control	46
First Steps with TensorFlow	48
Building Simple Models With Scikit-learn	49
Using NLTK for Sentiment Analysis	52
Chapter 3 Self-Assessment	54

4. ETHICAL AI ... 55
- Privacy Concerns ... 58
- Avoiding Bias ... 60
- AI and Job Displacement: Finding a Balance ... 61
- Risks and Responsibilities in Law Enforcement ... 63
- Future Ethical Challenges ... 64
- Keeping AI on Track ... 65
- Chapter 4 Self-Assessment ... 66

5. AI-ENHANCED CREATIVITY AND INNOVATION ... 69
- Generative Art ... 69
- The Art of the Prompt ... 71
- Writing with AI ... 74
- AI in Music Composition ... 76
- AI in Game Development ... 77
- Meet Ai-Da ... 78
- Innovating with AI ... 79
- Chapter 5 Self-Assessment ... 80

6. CAREER PATHWAYS IN AI ... 81
- The Importance of AI Literacy ... 81
- Transitioning into a Career in AI ... 82
- Exploring AI Jobs ... 83
- Essential Skills for AI Careers ... 86
- Networking in the AI Community ... 87
- Preparing for AI Job Interviews ... 88
- Chapter 6 Self-Assessment ... 92

7. A JOURNEY OF LIFELONG LEARNING ... 93
- Why Lifelong Learning Matters ... 93
- Time Management for Busy Learners ... 96
- Tips and Tricks to Stay Motivated ... 98
- Chapter 7 Self-Assessment ... 99

8. AI MISUNDERSTOOD ... 100
- Common Misconceptions About AI ... 100
- Chapter 8 Self-Assessment ... 105

9. PREPARING FOR THE FUTURE ... 106
- Emerging Trends: What's Next? ... 106
- AI for a Smarter, Safer, and More Sustainable Future ... 109

Building Resilience in an AI-Driven World	115
Chapter 9 Self-Assessment	116
Conclusion	117
References	121

INTRODUCTION

From the moment you wake up, AI is in the background, ready to make your day a little easier. Your smartphone greets you with a tailored weather report based on where you are and what's on your schedule, helping you plan your day. As you check your phone, news alerts and social media updates pop up, personalized to your interests, activities, and content you've previously liked. By lunchtime, as you scroll through your apps, it's almost as if the digital world knows you better than your best friend does, with each post and ad reflecting your interests, needs, and desires. After work, as you head to the grocery store to stock up for the next few days, AI steps in again, compiling grocery deals based on your past shopping habits, offering discounts on things you might need or may want to try. And, later in the evening, as you sink into your couch for much-needed downtime at the end of a busy day, the streaming service on your TV suggests shows based on your viewing history. Even as you drift off to sleep, AI keeps working, tracking your sleep patterns to suggest ways to improve your rest. These seemingly small, everyday conveniences show how deeply AI is embedded in our lives.

Welcome to Essentials of AI for Beginners, where your journey into this fascinating topic begins. It's my honor to serve as your knowledgeable companion as you explore the intriguing world of AI. My goals for this book are simple: to provide a straightforward and accessible guide to AI for beginners and to provide you with the information and guidance you need to embrace artificial intelligence and use it to reach your objectives. Whether you'd like to advance your career, explore your creative side, find new hobbies, stay relevant in the digital era, or prepare for success in the age of computer-generated reasoning, decision-making, and problem-solving, I'm here to educate, empower, and encourage you every step of the way.

These days, most people need to be familiar with AI, as it is rapidly becoming a necessary skill. Understanding how to navigate this ever-changing landscape can provide new opportunities and help you stay ahead, but it can also seem daunting. Rest assured that learning about AI doesn't have to be overwhelming; it can be fun, enjoyable, and accessible, and this book aims to demonstrate just that. If you think about learning AI as learning about a collection of tools, one tool at a time, and then using your newfound knowledge of those tools to build a new deck or construct a backyard shed that will add value to your home, it will help you see AI as a topic within reach, something that will benefit your life tremendously, and add value to your personal and professional pursuits.

This book is ideal for those who are curious about AI and want to explore it but need help determining where to begin. Maybe you've encountered terms like machine learning, generative AI, or ChatGPT and felt overwhelmed by this new language. Perhaps you're interested in using the power of AI to boost your creativity or advance your career but feel discouraged because you don't have a background in coding, data science, or advanced mathematics, or you don't feel there are enough hours in the day to learn with all your other responsibilities. Possibly, you're interested in conversing with your kids or grandkids about the technologies and AI tools they're immersed in, but you don't feel you have the language or sufficient understanding of the topic to engage them properly in conversation. Maybe you have concerns about AI due to the discussions surrounding its potential to replace humans in various fields or worry that its creation and implementation could be more responsible and ethical.

If you see yourself in any of these scenarios, you've come to the right place. This book will help address all these situations and more. I want you to feel supported in your learning journey and assure you that you're not alone. You possess the ability to comprehend, utilize, and enjoy AI!

> You can learn new things at any time in your life if you're willing to be a beginner. If you actually learn to like being a beginner, the whole world opens up to you.
>
> BARBARA SHER

Before we embark on this AI learning journey together, I'd like to introduce myself. Professionally, I bring over two decades of leadership experience in the private and non-profit sectors across Canada and the United States. I've worked with clients and partners worldwide, helping them achieve their goals by applying industry best practices and the latest innovations. Throughout my career, I've enjoyed being at the forefront of advancements—whether as an early adopter of new technologies, breaking barriers, or forging new paths. My recent deep engagement with AI reflects my pattern of embracing innovations with enthusiasm, and it has elevated both my work and personal life.

On a personal level, I've taken on new and unconventional challenges from a young age. As a preteen, I fought for the right to play hockey in a boys' league when no opportunities existed for girls (at that time, girls were directed towards ringette, not hockey). At 16, I became one of the first teenagers in my hometown to embark on a year-long student exchange to Germany—partly to learn a new language, partly for adventure, and partly to experience the European way of life. In university, I studied business, and for one semester, I studied in the German-speaking part of Switzerland, where I completed coursework, assignments, exams, and presentations in German, putting my informally acquired language skills to the test!

I've also become a certified rescue SCUBA diver, traveled to more than 40 countries, and lived and worked in Tanzania as part of a pilot program, where I conducted a business assessment of a national park in Zanzibar. That experience, which involved engaging extensively with local communities, sparked my passion for empowering others through education and entrepreneurship.

Given all this, not much scares or intimidates me. So, when AI began to penetrate various aspects of life and work, I embraced it with the same enthusiasm and determination I've applied to other challenges. These experiences have shaped my personal growth and my approach to innovation and problem-solving.

Embracing technology and developing innovative tools and frameworks has been central to my success. This expertise has helped me deliver tailored solutions for organizational challenges across industries such as education, healthcare, infrastructure, real estate, and regulation.

In recent years, AI has become my next frontier. Incorporating artificial intelligence into my work has sharpened the insights I deliver to clients and streamlined my workflows. It has also given me back valuable time—time I now use to pursue hobbies, travel, and spend more meaningful moments with my family. AI has been a game-changer in my professional and personal life, and I'm excited to share this journey with you.

This book isn't just about introducing you to the basics of AI; it's about making AI accessible and showing you how this technology can transform how you work, think, create, and live—just as it has for me.

So, what is AI?

Since this is a book about artificial intelligence, I asked ChatGPT—a leading AI chatbot that can interact with users in natural language—to define AI in beginner terms. Here's our text conversation:

INTRODUCTION　　　　　　　　　　　　　　　　xv

> I'm writing a book on AI for people new to the topic. Please provide a definition of AI that beginners will understand. Thanks!

> Artificial Intelligence (AI) is a type of technology that allows machines, like computers, to perform tasks that would normally require human intelligence. This can include things like recognizing speech, understanding language, solving problems, or even learning from experience. Think of it as teaching a machine to act and make decisions like a human, but much faster and often with the ability to process more information at once.

The response provided by ChatGPT is spot-on and a small illustration of the tool's robustness. While it's unnecessary to say 'please' and 'thank you' to ChatGPT, I sometimes do because of its human-like conversational style. So, I communicate with it much like talking to a friend.

How is this book structured?

The book is designed to guide you through AI in a clear and accessible way, supporting your journey from a foundational understanding of key concepts and terminology to active engagement through hands-on activities.

Throughout this book, you'll find several QR codes that can be scanned with a smartphone for quick access to digital content. If you'd prefer to view the digital content on a computer instead of a smartphone, shortened links that are easy and intuitive to enter into your browser are also provided. The digital content that comes with this book includes:

- Several step-by-step tutorials to aid you in building your first applications and generating your first AI images.
- End-of-chapter quizzes to reinforce learning.

- Bonus material that includes descriptions of and use cases for over 30 popular AI tools and platforms.
- A comprehensive glossary of terms.

Essentials of AI for Beginners includes many case studies and real-world examples of AI. It's important to know that the case studies are fictional. Actual uses of AI inspire them, but the names, businesses, and other details are created for illustrative purposes only and should not be interpreted as real-life examples.

Although all chapters are valuable, I acknowledge that not everyone has identical learning goals or interests in AI. For this reason, I've developed personalized learning tracks to cater to individual preferences and assist you in prioritizing what is most important to you. First, here's a brief overview of each chapter:

1. **AI Fundamentals:** Introduces vital terminology and concepts, providing a solid foundation for success.
2. **Practical Applications of AI:** Showcases real-world applications of AI use in different sectors and contexts.
3. **Hands-on Exploration of AI:** Provides step-by-step tutorials to implement AI terminology and core concepts.
4. **Ethical AI:** Recognizes and addresses concerns regarding the ethical and responsible use of AI.
5. **AI-Enhanced Creativity and Innovation:** Highlights uses of AI to boost creativity and drive innovation.
6. **Career Pathways in AI:** Explores how AI can enhance your career.
7. **A Journey of Lifelong Learning:** Encourages a commitment to ongoing learning to stay ahead.
8. **AI Misunderstood:** Dispels common misconceptions about AI.
9. **Preparing for the Future:** Explores emerging trends in AI.

Now that we're familiar with each chapter's content, here are four personalized learning tracks designed to meet different learning goals.

Learning Track 1: Practical Applications

This track is ideal for those seeking hands-on guidance in developing AI models and applications, integrating AI into everyday tasks, and using AI in creative endeavors.

- **Essential chapters:** 1, 2, 3, and 5.
- **Recommended chapters:** 4 and 7.
- **Optional chapters:** 6, 8, and 9.

Learning Track 2: Career Enhancement

This track is targeted at professionals seeking to use AI for career advancement. Explore AI's application across healthcare, finance, education, and more industries. Gain insights into acquiring AI skills, understanding industry trends, and positioning oneself as an asset in an AI-influenced job market.

- **Essential chapters:** 1, 2, 3, 5, 6, and 7.
- **Recommended chapters:** 4.
- **Optional chapters:** 8 and 9.

Learning Track 3: Creative Applications

This track is designed for those who want to skip coding and instead focus on "ready-made" AI tools and applications to enhance their creative pursuits, such as creating art, composing music, writing novels, and more.

- **Essential chapters:** 1, 2, and 5.
- **Recommended chapters:** 4 and 7.
- **Optional chapters:** 3, 6, 8 and 9.

Learning Track 4: Theoretical Foundations

This track explores the core principles and theories for those intrigued by AI, including machine learning algorithms, neural networks, and data analysis. It provides a deep, conceptual understanding of AI's workings, appealing to those who value knowledge of the underlying principles and motivations behind its functionality.

- **Essential chapters:** 1, 2, and 4.
- **Recommended chapters:** 3, 5, 8 and 9.
- **Optional chapters:** 6 and 7.

Engaging with this book offers several tangible benefits. First, you'll gain a solid understanding of AI fundamentals and their practical applications in everyday life. Second, you'll develop valuable skills to utilize AI tools and technologies effectively. Third, it will inspire you to explore new creative possibilities. Finally, you'll build the confidence to stay ahead of the latest innovations in this rapidly evolving field.

You're about to embark on an exciting journey of discovery, empowerment, and personal growth. This book is your reliable guide, and I'm here to support you every step of the way. Rest assured that even if certain concepts seem difficult initially, with determination and a sense of curiosity, you'll undoubtedly achieve success.

Alright, let's get started. Dive in, explore, and see how AI has the potential to change your life.

ONE
AI FUNDAMENTALS

Artificial Intelligence (AI) is pervasive, factoring into many aspects of our lives, sometimes without us even realizing it. Therefore, we should all have some degree of literacy in this topic. Understanding core AI-related terms and concepts is necessary for deeper exploration of this topic and its practical applications in our increasingly digital world, just like knowing the materials needed and the construction methods to follow while building a house.

Having an appreciation of how things work helps in numerous ways. It will enable you to contribute thoughtfully and confidently during AI discussions, whether discussing potential applications of the technology and its impacts and benefits with colleagues, friends, and family or conversing about the subject with peers at conferences and networking events. It will enable you to comprehend better and appreciate the content of AI-related articles, books, videos, and other materials. Also, it will help you ask appropriate questions, find relevant information, and make informed decisions about implementing AI in your personal or professional life.

ARTIFICIAL INTELLIGENCE EXPLAINED

AI simulates human intelligence processes by machines, particularly computer systems. These processes include learning (acquiring information and rules for using it), reasoning (using the rules to reach approximate or definite conclusions), and self-correction (learning from mistakes and continually striving to improve).

At its core, AI involves creating algorithms that enable machines to undertake tasks that usually require human intelligence. An algorithm is a set of rules or instructions given to a computer or AI system to help it solve problems or make decisions. Consider this sequential algorithm for making a tomato and cheese sandwich.

1. Gather ingredients and tools.
   - Two slices of bread.
   - One slice of cheese.
   - One slice of tomato.
   - Butter.
   - A knife.
2. Prepare the bread.
   - Take two slices of bread and place them on a plate.
3. Spread the butter.
   - Spread the butter on one side of each slice of bread using the knife.
4. Add the cheese.
   - Place the cheese slice on the buttered side of one slice of bread.
5. Add the tomato.
   - Place the slice of tomato on top of the cheese.
6. Close the sandwich.
   - Place the second slice of bread on top of the tomato, with the buttered side facing inward.
7. Cut the sandwich.
   - Use the knife to cut the sandwich in half.
8. Serve.

Sequential algorithms follow a precise, ordered sequence, simply moving from one step to the next. Given the same ingredients and following the steps, the outcome—a tomato and cheese sandwich—will be the same every time.

These algorithms are just one of many types, and they can be broadly categorized into three main groups: purpose-based, strategy-based, and learning-based algorithms.

Purpose-based algorithms are classified based on the specific tasks or problems they're designed to solve. You'd choose a purpose-based algorithm based on what you want to achieve, such as searching for information, sorting data, compressing data for more accessible storage and transmission, solving problems related to graphs, or optimizing a solution. Given this description, these examples of purpose-based algorithms won't surprise you. They include search, sorting, graph, optimization, and compression algorithms.

Strategy-based algorithms are categorized based on their approach or method to solve problems, such as how the algorithm operates. Divide-and-conquer algorithms are one example of a strategy-based algorithm. They solve a problem by breaking it into smaller subproblems, solving each independently, and then combining the results. Another example of a strategy-based algorithm is a sequential algorithm, like the one used to make a tomato and cheese sandwich. You'd choose a strategy-based algorithm that best fits the nature of the problem you're trying to solve and the constraints you're working within.

Learning-based algorithms are designed to learn from data, improving their performance over time as they process more information. Subclassifications of learning-based algorithms include supervised learning algorithms, unsupervised learning algorithms, and reinforcement learning algorithms. This classification and subclassification of algorithms are essential in machine learning and AI, as they guide the choice of algorithms based on available data and the specific problem they are meant to address.

Let's examine this concept further with an example: deciding whether to go outside to garden. There are three factors to consider when making a decision: weather (sunny, rainy, overcast), temperature (hot, mild, cool), and humidity (high, normal). This problem can be solved using a decision tree algorithm, a supervised learning algorithm that makes decisions based on certain factors or conditions. Here's how it might work:

- Start with the weather.
    - If it's sunny, check the humidity.
        - If the humidity is high, don't garden.
        - If the humidity is normal, garden.
    - If it's overcast, garden (regardless of humidity or temperature).
    - If it's rainy, check the temperature.
        - If the temperature is cool, don't garden.
        - If the temperature is mild or hot, garden.

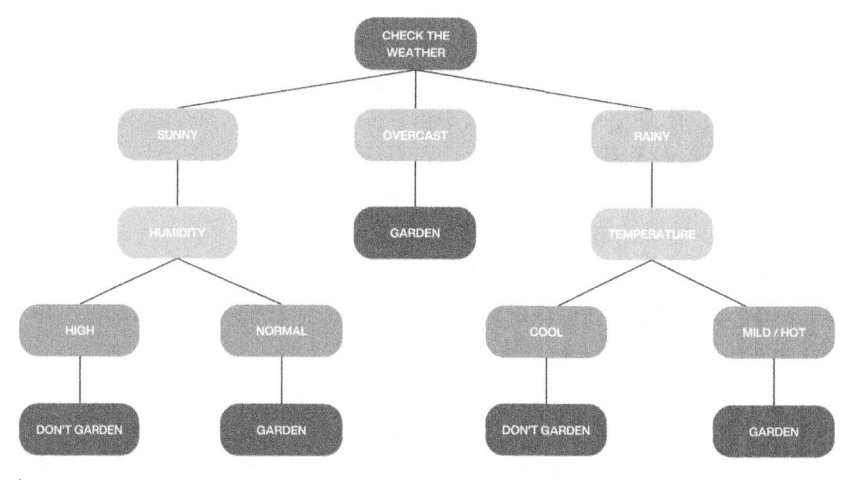

A visual representation of a decision tree algorithm to help you decide whether to garden. Created in Canva.

AI differs from other technologies due to its unique ability to adapt and improve. Traditional programming relies on explicit instructions by humans detailing each step required to perform a task. In contrast, AI systems learn from data and adapt their behavior without explicit programming for every scenario. This adaptability enables AI to excel in complex and dynamic environments, making it a powerful tool across various fields.

Virtual assistants like Siri and Alexa use AI to understand and respond to voice commands. They can set reminders, answer questions, and control connected home devices such as lighting systems, thermostats, door locks, security systems, garage door openers, and more. The AI-powered online recommendation systems used by Amazon and Netflix analyze user behavior to suggest products or movies tailored to individual preferences. AI-powered chatbots in customer service provide instant responses to common queries, improving customer satisfaction and efficiency. Social media platforms utilize AI to curate content, ensuring users see posts – and advertisements – that align with their interests and online searching habits. In smartphones, AI enhances features like facial recognition and photo editing.

How exactly does AI work?

As we've learned, algorithms lie at the heart of AI, playing a crucial role in problem-solving and decision-making processes. Learning-based algorithms, such as neural networks, enable AI systems to perform tasks ranging from simple data sorting to intricate image recognition.

Different types of AI algorithms cater to various needs and applications. For example, a linear regression model, a type of supervised learning algorithm, might analyze historical data on house prices and features—such as size, location, number of bedrooms, and proximity to schools and other community amenities—to predict house prices.

Unsupervised learning algorithms like K-means clustering work with unlabeled data to find hidden patterns. A retail store, for example, could use K-means clustering to segment customers based on purchasing behavior, enabling personalized marketing strategies. In simple terms, K-means clustering is a machine learning method that groups data into clusters (or groups) based on their similarities. The algorithm groups similar data points by placing a centroid (a center point or cluster center) in each cluster and then assigning each point to the closest centroid, adjusting the centroids until they best represent their clusters. In the end, you'll have clusters where similar data points are grouped together, making it easier to see patterns or trends.

TEACHING MACHINES TO LEARN

Machine learning (ML) is a vital subset of AI. It involves training computers to learn from data so they improve over time without needing specific instructions for each task. Think of it as the difference between instructing a child step-by-step on tying their shoes versus showing them various methods and letting them figure out the most straightforward way through practice.

The data processing pipeline is central to machine learning. It begins with data collection, where relevant information is gathered from various sources. This data often requires processing to remove inconsistencies and errors, like 'cleaning' the data before it's used. Feature extraction and selection follow, meaning essential characteristics of the data are identified and chosen for analysis. Next, the data is used to train the model, where the AI system learns to make decisions or predictions (like predicting whether a piece of fruit is an apple or orange based on features like color and weight). Finally, model evaluation follows, testing the model's accuracy and fine-tuning it for better performance.

To reinforce how machine learning works, let's briefly revisit the concepts of supervised and unsupervised learning; the former involves training a model on a labeled dataset, meaning the data comes with correct answers, while the latter deals with unlabeled data, requiring the model to find hidden patterns or groupings without prior knowledge of what it should be looking for.

Real-world examples of machine learning are plentiful. In manufacturing, for example, predictive maintenance systems analyze data from machinery to foresee potential failures and schedule timely repairs. Banks use machine learning to detect fraudulent transactions by analyzing your spending patterns and flagging any unusual activity, such as purchases made abroad when you're sitting at home or for unusually large amounts. Airlines, ride-sharing services, and hotels use dynamic pricing models, where machine learning algorithms analyze factors like demand, booking patterns, and even weather to adjust prices in real-time to maximize revenue while offering competitive pricing to customers. Farmers use AI to analyze soil conditions and weather patterns to optimize crop yields. Social media platforms employ image recognition to tag photos automatically to enhance the user experience, and they also use machine learning to identify and remove inappropriate content, such as hate speech, disinformation, and harmful or graphic images. Common misconceptions about machine learning often blur its distinction from AI. While machine learning is a crucial component of AI, it doesn't encompass all AI applications. Furthermore, machine learning systems do not always require human intervention at every phase. Once trained, these models can operate autonomously, continuously learning and adapting based on new data.

MIMICKING THE HUMAN BRAIN

Neural networks simulate the function and structure of the human brain and form the basis of many AI applications. These systems consist of layers of interconnected nodes, or "neurons," which process data like how biological neurons transmit signals. Each neuron receives input, performs a computation, and passes the result to the next layer. This layered approach allows neural networks to learn and recognize intricate patterns in data, making them incredibly powerful for tasks like image recognition and language processing.

Nodes, layers, and weights are at the core of a neural network's structure. Nodes, or artificial neurons, are the fundamental units processing input data spread out across layers. Layers are collections of these nodes arranged in an input layer, at least one hidden layer (often more), and an output layer. The input layer takes in raw data, such as pixel values from an image, while the hidden layers perform complex computations to extract features and patterns. The output layer then produces the result, such as identifying the object in the image. A neural network can have many layers but at minimum three: one input layer, one hidden layer, and one output layer. Weights are the adjustable parameters that determine the strength of connections between nodes, like synapses in the human brain. They are modified during training to improve the network's accuracy.

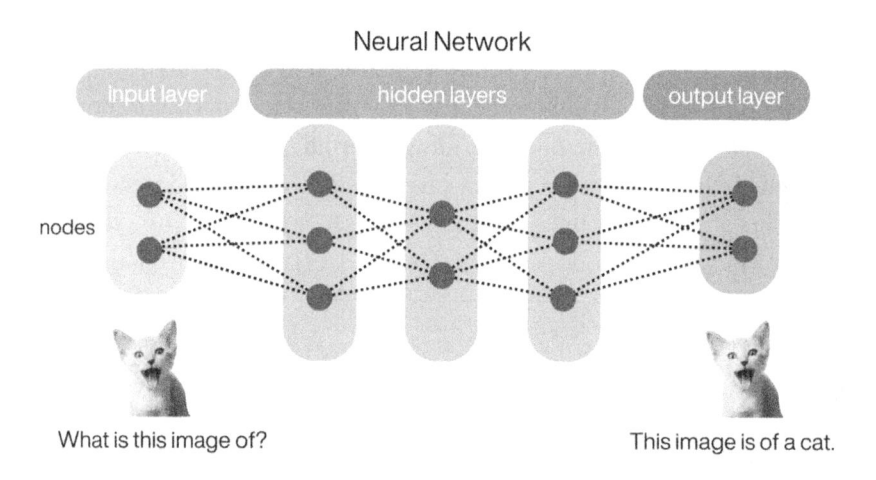

Neural Network

A visual representation of a neural network used to recognize images, with one input layer, three hidden layers, and one output layer. Designed in Canva.

Since neural networks are foundational to AI and different types of neural networks are mentioned throughout this book, let's explore some of the most common types in greater detail.

A Feedforward Neural Network (FNN) allows information to flow in only one direction—from the input nodes through the hidden nodes to the output nodes. This type of neural network does not have cycles or loops, hence the name "feedforward."

A good example of an FNN is having a list of ingredients and the amount of each and trying to determine whether you can bake a cake with them. You input your ingredients, like flour, sugar, and eggs, into the network. The network processes these inputs in layers, making simple decisions at each step, like "Is there enough sugar?" Finally, the network decides: "Yes, you can bake a cake" or "No, you cannot."

In this example, the input layer is your ingredient list. The hidden layers are the decision-making steps, such as checking the ingredients and the quantities of each. The output layer is the final decision—whether you can bake a cake with the ingredients you have.

A Convolutional Neural Network (CNN) analyzes visual data. Unlike a Feedforward Neural Network, which looks at the entire input simultaneously, a CNN processes small portions of the input at a time. This helps the network recognize patterns and then combine these patterns to understand the whole image.

To explain this concept further, let's use the example of putting a puzzle together. Instead of looking at the picture on the box, you start by closely examining each piece. As you do this, you notice some pieces have green edges (which could be grass), and some have blue edges (which could be sky). As you continue examining each piece, you start to put the pieces together, recognizing the larger picture, which, in this example, is a landscape.

The convolutional layers in our puzzle example can be equated to the steps you took to examine each piece to identify colors, shapes, and patterns. Pooling layers help you simplify your puzzle by focusing on the most essential pieces and ignoring unnecessary details. Fully connected layers (or dense layers) enable you to combine the pieces to recognize the entire image once you've examined all the pieces.

A Recurrent Neural Network (RNN) handles data in sequences, such as sentences, time series, or any data where the order matters. RNNs are unique because they have a "memory" that helps them keep track of previous inputs, allowing them to consider the context when making decisions.

Consider how you read a story. As you read one sentence at a time, you don't look at each in isolation to understand it. Instead, you remember what happened in previous sentences. For example, if the story says, "The cat chased the mouse," and then later mentions, "It caught it," you know the first "it" refers to the cat, and the second "it" refers to the mouse because you remember the earlier sentence.

In our story example, the "input" is each sentence in the story, "memory" is your ability to remember what happened earlier, and the "output" is your understanding of the story as it unfolds. This is how RNNs work, and they are beneficial for tasks such as language translation, speech recognition, or predicting the next word in a text.

The last type of neural network we'll examine is a Generative Adversarial Network (GAN). GANs have two networks that work against each other (hence the term "adversarial") to create something new. One tries to create fake data, while the other tries to detect if the data is fake or real. Over time, both networks get better: the generator of the "fake data" makes more realistic data, and the discriminator becomes better at spotting fakes.

Let's explore this concept further. You are learning to draw portraits. You draw a picture and then show it to a friend with excellent attention to detail who's good at spotting mistakes. Your friend tells you what looks fake or "off " about your drawing, so you try to improve it. Over time, in attempting to fool your friend, you get better at drawing realistic portraits.

In this example, you are the "generator," the network trying to create images that look real, and your friend is the "discriminator," the network trying to figure out if the image produced is real or fake. This is how GANs work. The generator creates data, and the discriminator checks if it's real or fake. As they both improve over time, the generator produces ever-more realistic outputs, often making it difficult to tell the difference between what is real and what is generated.

GOING DEEPER WITH AI

Deep learning (DL), an advanced form of machine learning, involves numerous layers of artificial neurons, each building on the knowledge gained from previous layers to make sense of complex data. This hierarchical approach allows deep learning models to excel at tasks requiring high-level abstraction, such as human speech recognition or recognizing objects in images. Shallow layers identify simple edges and textures in image recognition, while deeper layers recognize shapes, objects, and scenes.

Deep learning has abundant and transformative real-world applications. It powers virtual assistants in speech recognition, enabling them to understand and respond to natural language queries. These systems analyze the nuances of speech, including accents and intonations, to provide accurate responses. In natural language processing (NLP), deep learning algorithms enhance machine translation services, making it possible to translate text between languages with remarkable accuracy. NLP models like the latest GPT-4 generate human-like text, aiding content creation and customer service.

Deep learning is driving innovations that were once in the realm of science fiction. Autonomous vehicles, for instance, use deep learning to interpret sensor data, make real-time decisions, and navigate safely. Healthcare benefits from deep learning through diagnostic tools that analyze medical images, identifying anomalies with greater precision than human doctors. Robots in warehouses or manufacturing plants use deep learning models to recognize and pick up objects, navigate environments, and perform tasks with precision. As technology evolves, deep learning applications will expand, offering new possibilities and reshaping our world.

AI'S TRIO: ML, NN, AND DL

Machine learning (ML) is a subset of AI that, as we've learned, enables computers to learn from data. Central to machine learning are neural networks (NN). Neural networks are the foundation for deep learning (DL), a more advanced subset of machine learning that uses multiple layers of neurons to extract features from data. These relationships can be compared to a set of nested dolls, where deep learning is nestled within neural networks, which are nestled within machine learning, and within the broader field of AI.

ARTIFICIAL INTELLIGENCE   MACHINE LEARNING   NEURAL NETWORKS   DEEP LEARNING

Four nested dolls illustrate the relationships between AI, machine learning, neural networks, and deep learning. Image generated on the OpenArt platform using Stable Diffusion model 3.0, and edited in Canva.

Practical examples help further illustrate these differences. Basic classification tasks, such as determining whether an email is spam, often rely on traditional machine learning algorithms like logistic regression or decision trees, which are sufficient for simple tasks involving structured data. However, when it comes to complex pattern recognition, such as identifying objects in images or understanding natural language, deep learning models like convolutional neural networks (CNNs) and recurrent neural networks (RNNs) are necessary. These models excel in handling unstructured data and extracting intricate patterns through their multiple layers of neurons.

THE AI SPECTRUM: NARROW TO SUPER AI

Narrow AI, or Weak AI, performs specific tasks without possessing general intelligence. Narrow AI is a practical and widely deployed system that makes everyday activities more efficient and personalized. These AI systems excel in particular domains but cannot perform tasks outside their specialization. For instance, recommendation engines on platforms like Netflix, YouTube, and Amazon analyze user preferences to suggest movies or products, but they cannot perform unrelated tasks like setting reminders and providing weather updates.

General AI or Artificial General Intelligence (AGI) is more robust than narrow AI. True AGI remains a theoretical concept that envisions an AI that can reason and solve problems across various domains (like humans) and exhibit emotional intelligence. While AGI is not yet here, some experts argue the most important elements of general AI have been or are very close to being achieved by some of today's most advanced large language models (LLM), such as ChatGPT and Claude, two popular chatbots. Achieving AGI presents challenges, including the need for more advanced machine learning algorithms, vast amounts of data, and computational power. Also, ethical considerations arise, such as ensuring these systems operate within moral and societal norms.

Super AI, or Artificial Superintelligence, remains speculative and refers to AI that surpasses human intelligence in all aspects. This type of AI would perform tasks more efficiently, generate new ideas, create art, and even innovate beyond human capabilities. The speculative nature of Super AI invites theoretical discussions about its implications for humanity. Questions arise about the ethical use of such powerful technology and its impact on society. For instance, could Super AI solve global challenges like climate change or pose difficult-to-foresee risks?

Comparing these types of AI highlights Narrow AI's current practicality and widespread use, General AI's ambitious goals, and Super AI's speculative future, each offering unique insights and challenges.

SIMPLE ALGORITHMS TO ADVANCED SYSTEMS

You may be surprised to learn that the concept of AI has existed since the 1940s. Neuroscientist Warren McCulloch and logician Walter Pitts laid the foundation for AI in their 1943 work *A Logical Calculus of Ideas Immanent in Nervous Activity*, in which they proposed a model of artificial neurons, an early attempt to simulate the brain's processes using mathematical models, signifying the beginning of neural network theory, which remains crucial in AI today.

Then came along Alan Turing, a British mathematician and logician, often regarded as the father of modern computer science. During World War II, he was one of the top-secret codebreakers at London's Bletchley Park. There, he decrypted ciphers generated by Germany's Enigma machine, which was considered unbreakable. Turing's work not only influenced cryptography but also provided the basis for computational thinking. After the war in 1950, Turing introduced the Turing Test, a mental exercise to determine whether a computer could pass as a human, laying the foundation for AI as we know it today. An exciting way to learn more about Turing and his work is by watching the 2014 thriller/war movie "Imitation Game" based on his biography.

My earliest experience with computer programming was in high school when I learned the Turing programming language. Turing was widely used in high schools and universities as an introduction to programming, as its syntax is intuitive and readable. Object-oriented Turing and Turing+ are variations of the original or classic Turing language I learned. While Alan Turing did not invent this language, his contributions to the field of computer science inspired two University of Toronto faculty members to develop it in 1982 and name it after him.

Many consider the AI journey to have begun at the Dartmouth Conference in 1956, but as we've learned, the concept of AI originated in the minds of humans much earlier. The Dartmouth Conference was a historic event as brilliant minds in mathematics, computer science, and electrical engineering, including John McCarthy, Marvin Minsky, and Claude Shannon, convened to discuss the potential of building machines that could mimic human intelligence. This conference laid the groundwork for AI as a formal field of study, introducing foundational concepts that would steer decades of research and development.

The 1970s and 1980s saw the rise of expert systems, which marked a significant advancement in AI applications. These systems used rule-based algorithms to mimic the decision-making abilities of human experts. For instance, MYCIN, developed at Stanford University, could diagnose bacterial infections and recommend treatments. Expert systems found applications in various fields, from medical diagnostics to financial analysis, showcasing AI's potential to augment human expertise. While these early systems were limited to narrow domains, they demonstrated AI's promise in automating complex, rule-based tasks, setting the stage for more sophisticated systems in the future.

One of the most notable milestones in AI history is the development of IBM's Watson. In 2011, Watson competed on the quiz show Jeopardy! against two of the show's greatest champions, Ken Jennings and Brad Rutter. Watson's ability to understand and respond to natural language questions and its vast knowledge base allowed it to outperform its human competitors. This achievement highlighted the leaps made in natural language processing and machine learning, demonstrating AI's capability to handle unstructured data and complex queries. Watson's success illustrated AI's potential in entertainment and hinted at its broader applications in fields like healthcare, where natural language understanding is crucial.

These milestones reflect the rapid evolution of AI, from theoretical discussions to practical applications that enhance our daily lives. As AI advances as it inevitably will, it promises even more significant innovations, reshaping industries and redefining what machines can achieve.

* * *

CHAPTER 1 SELF-ASSESSMENT

Ready to test your knowledge? Scan the following QR code to take a multiple-choice quiz or enter this URL in your browser [**https://tinyurl.com/AICh1Quiz**]. It's a fun way to reinforce what you've learned and only takes a few minutes.

QR code for the Chapter 1 quiz.

TWO
PRACTICAL APPLICATIONS OF AI

When you visit your doctor today, you'll encounter a mix of human care and cutting-edge tech. This isn't a future vision—it's happening now, powered by AI.

Healthcare is changing fast, with AI advancements leading the charge. It can accurately and quickly diagnose diseases, create personalized treatment plans, and simplify administrative tasks. The result? Better, faster care that benefits both patients and providers. AI isn't just streamlining healthcare—it's reshaping and modernizing it.

The impact and influence of AI reaches well beyond the medical field. In the financial services industry, AI is revolutionizing how we handle and engage with our finances. Gone are the days of enduring lengthy waits at bank branches or spending hours on the phone for routine transactions. AI has fundamentally changed how businesses provide customer service, detect fraud, and offer investment strategies. With the help of sophisticated chatbots, round-the-clock customer support is now available. Fraud detection systems have become more robust, ensuring the safety of your assets. Additionally, AI-powered robo-advisors provide personalized investment strategies tailored to your needs. It's like having a highly knowledgeable financial assistant at your disposal, always ready to help with a wide range of financial tasks and decisions.

In this chapter, we'll explore the various applications of AI in healthcare and finance, retail and e-commerce, entertainment, education, and more. By examining these sectors, you'll discover how and to what extent AI is shaping our world, opening new possibilities, and tackling intricate challenges.

HEALTHCARE INNOVATIONS AND IMPACTS

AI's role in healthcare is vast and varied, and a great starting point to understanding its power is with diagnostic innovations. One of the most significant advancements is medical imaging, where AI algorithms analyze radiology scans to detect tumors and other abnormalities. These systems can identify minuscule details that might be invisible to the human eye, leading to earlier and more accurate diagnoses. For instance, AI can highlight suspicious areas in mammograms, increasing early-stage breast cancer detection rates. This saves lives and reduces the need for invasive biopsies and additional tests.

Another groundbreaking application is AI-powered predictive analytics for early disease detection. By analyzing enormous amounts of patient data, AI can detect trends and risk factors that could signal the onset of diseases like diabetes or cardiovascular conditions. These predictive models enable doctors to intervene sooner, offering preventive treatments and lifestyle recommendations. By taking a proactive approach, healthcare is transformed from a reactive to a preventive paradigm, lessening the overall strain on healthcare systems and improving patient satisfaction and outcomes.

AI also influences personalized medicine. Traditionally, treatments have followed a one-size-fits-all approach, but AI enables a more tailored strategy for the individual. In genomics, AI analyzes genetic information to create personalized treatment plans. Understanding a patient's unique genetic makeup enables doctors to prescribe medications that are most likely to be effective. AI also identifies optimal drug combinations, minimizing side effects and enhancing treatment efficacy. This customization ensures patients receive the best care based on their needs.

Surgical robots, guided by AI algorithms, enhance precision in complex procedures, allowing surgeons to perform minimally invasive surgeries more accurately. These robots can execute movements with steadiness and precision, often surpassing human capabilities, reducing surgical complications and faster patient recovery times.

In rehabilitation, AI-driven robotic exoskeletons help patients with mobility challenges regain function, provide personalized assistance, and track progress over time. Additionally, autonomous robots are being deployed in hospital settings for tasks such as medication delivery, disinfection, and even patient monitoring, reducing the risk of infections and freeing healthcare workers to focus on more complex patient care tasks.

Beyond direct patient care, AI streamlines numerous administrative tasks. For instance, AI systems manage patient appointments by analyzing schedules and optimizing booking times, reducing wait times and improving clinic efficiency. In billing and coding, AI automates translating medical records into billing codes, reducing errors and speeding up reimbursement, providing healthcare professionals more time to focus on patient care.

These advancements illustrate the powerful potential of AI in healthcare, from enhancing diagnostic accuracy to personalizing treatments and optimizing administrative tasks.

Case Study: Gayle's Early Cancer Detection

Gayle Williams, a 46-year-old marketing executive and mother of three, prioritized her health. Despite no family history of breast cancer, the diagnosis of two close friends strengthened her commitment to regular screenings. In 2022, during her routine mammogram, an AI-enhanced imaging system analyzed her results. The AI, trained on millions of mammogram images, detected the tiniest abnormality a standard review could have easily missed. Alerted by the AI, the radiologist re-examined the scans and recommended a biopsy. Thanks to the AI's early detection, doctors caught Gayle's cancer at Stage 1, with no lymph node involvement. This early intervention allowed her to undergo less aggressive treatment, avoid chemotherapy, and maintain a higher quality of life during recovery.

SHAPING MODERN BANKING

In banking and financial services, AI is transforming how institutions manage risk and ensure security. One of the most impactful applications is fraud detection, where AI analyzes massive amounts of transaction data to identify unusual patterns that may indicate fraudulent activities. These systems can detect and flag suspicious transactions for further investigation. For instance, if your credit card is suddenly used in a foreign country while you're making purchases at home, AI systems can instantly recognize this inconsistency and alert you or even freeze the account temporarily. This real-time monitoring significantly reduces the likelihood of fraud, protecting consumers and financial institutions.

AI in banking isn't only about consumer and institutional protection, though. AI also offers personalized financial services, tailoring advice and support to individual needs. Robo-advisors are a prime example of using AI to manage investment portfolios based on one's financial goals and risk tolerance. These digital advisors continuously monitor market conditions and adjust investments accordingly. In many cases, such robo-advisors can outperform human advisors due to their ability to swiftly process and analyze large datasets. Additionally, AI-powered chatbots in banking apps provide instant assistance with common queries, such as checking account balances. These chatbots are available 24 hours a day, 7 days a week, offering convenience that traditional customer service cannot match.

When it comes to loans and credit, AI also shines. AI algorithms look at much more than your credit score to determine whether you should receive a loan or a higher credit card limit. Many other factors are analyzed, such as your online social media activity, phone use, transaction history, and more, providing a bigger picture of who you are and what you do. A holistic view enhances AI's ability to provide more accurate assessments, leading to fewer defaults.

AI's impact on trading and investment is also profound, particularly in high-frequency trading. AI algorithms execute trades at lightning speed, far faster than you can blink, taking advantage of market inefficiencies that human traders might miss or spotting market trends before they fully emerge. These systems' ability to make such quick decisions can lead to significant gains.

AI tools for market sentiment analysis analyze news articles, social media chatter, and other information sources to gauge public sentiment about stocks and other financial instruments. This added layer of insight helps traders make more informed decisions based on the market's collective mood rather than only relying on numerical data.

Case Study: Mark's Road to Financial Optimization

Mark Quibble, a 35-year-old engineer, aimed to optimize his finances while managing responsibilities for his family and aging parents. He used AI tools for budgeting, bill optimization, automated savings, investment management, and credit score improvement. The AI apps helped him cut expenses, cancel unused subscriptions, and save more each month. He switched to a robo-advisor for his investment accounts, which regularly rebalanced his investments, optimizing them for his risk tolerance and retirement timeline. Additionally, an AI credit monitoring service gave him personalized suggestions to improve his credit score, leading to better terms on his mortgage refinance.

After eight months, Mark saved $2,640 through reduced expenses and automated savings. His investment returns improved, and his credit score rose by 40 points, saving him $45,000 in mortgage interest. He expects to retire four years early with an extra $220,000 in his retirement fund, giving him peace of mind for his family's future.

ENHANCING CUSTOMER EXPERIENCE IN RETAIL AND E-COMMERCE

In retail and e-commerce, AI is the unseen force that tailors your shopping experience to your unique preferences. One of the most noticeable applications is through recommendation engines on online retail platforms. These AI systems analyze your browsing history, purchase patterns, and even the time you spend looking at specific items. By processing this data, they suggest products that align with your tastes. For instance, if you frequently shop for fitness gear, the AI will recommend the latest running shoes or workout apparel. This personalized approach enhances your shopping experience and increases your likelihood of purchasing, which is excellent for business, not necessarily your wallet!

AI also revolutionizes inventory management, a critical aspect of retail operations. Predictive analytics enable retailers to forecast demand more accurately, ensuring that popular products are always in stock. For example, AI can predict which items will be more in demand in winter than in other seasons or during specific events by analyzing historical sales data, market trends, and social media buzz. This foresight allows retailers to adjust their stock levels proactively. Automated inventory replenishment systems further streamline this process by automatically placing orders for low-stock items, reducing the risk of stockouts and overstock situations. This optimization improves customer satisfaction and minimizes storage costs and waste.

AI is also altering retail customer service, mainly through chatbots. These agents handle customer inquiries around the clock, responding instantly to common questions about products, orders, and returns. By integrating natural language processing, these chatbots understand and respond to customer inquiries in a conversational manner, making interactions feel more personal.

Sentiment analysis adds another layer of sophistication, allowing retailers to gauge customer emotions through their interactions. This insight helps businesses identify areas for improvement and address customer concerns more effectively, enhancing overall satisfaction.

AI's impact extends to logistics and delivery, significantly boosting supply chain efficiency. By analyzing traffic patterns, weather conditions, and delivery schedules, AI algorithms optimize delivery routes, ensuring packages reach their destinations as quickly and cost-effectively as possible. Predictive maintenance for delivery vehicles further enhances efficiency by using AI to monitor vehicle health and forecast potential issues before they lead to breakdowns. This proactive approach minimizes downtime and ensures that deliveries remain on schedule, contributing to a smoother and more reliable supply chain.

Case Study: AI-Driven Improvement in Inventory Management for Exotic Pets

Exotic Pets, a family-owned retailer in Phoenix, Arizona, sells specialized products for exotic birds and reptiles. After expanding online, they faced challenges balancing in-store and online inventory. To address these issues, they integrated AI into their inventory management process. AI-driven business improvements included:

- *Tailored Demand Forecasting:* AI analyzed sales data, seasonal trends, and online shopping behaviors to predict demand for specific products, such as bird perches and reptile heating lamps.
- *Automated Stock Replenishment:* The AI system monitored inventory and initiated restocks for items like reptile food or bird cages when levels were low, ensuring stock availability.
- *Optimized Just-in-Time Delivery:* AI streamlined the delivery of high-demand items, reducing storage costs and ensuring timely in-store and online sales restocking.
- *Supplier Coordination:* Sharing AI forecasts with suppliers helped Exotic Pets reduce lead times for hard-to-find

items like custom reptile habitats, improving the supply chain.
- *Dynamic Pricing and Promotions:* AI suggested pricing and promotions based on real-time inventory and market trends, optimizing sales and managing overstock.

AI improved Exotic Pets' demand forecasting accuracy by 30%, reduced stockouts, and cut storage costs with optimized just-in-time delivery. This allowed the company to scale efficiently and continue providing specialized products to customers locally and across the U.S.

TRANSFORMING THE ENTERTAINMENT INDUSTRY

AI is changing the entertainment industry by enhancing creativity and personalizing user experiences. AI algorithms are becoming indispensable tools for artists and creators in content creation. These algorithms can generate unique music compositions and create stunning artwork, pushing the boundaries of human creativity. AI can compose movie background scores, generate visual art that captures the essence of a scene, or even assist in writing scripts. AI tools for scriptwriting analyze existing scripts to suggest plot twists and character arcs. At the same time, AI-powered video editing software can automatically cut and splice footage, saving hours of manual work.

Personalized content recommendations are another significant application of AI in entertainment. Streaming services like Netflix and Spotify use sophisticated recommendation engines to analyze your viewing or listening habits, suggesting content tailored to your preferences. These engines consider your past behavior, trending topics and songs, and even the time of day to offer personalized suggestions. On social media platforms, AI curates content that aligns with your interests, ensuring you see posts, videos, articles, and advertisements that are most relevant to you. This level of personalization enhances user engagement and satisfaction, making your entertainment experience more enjoyable.

AI also plays a vital part in developing more immersive and interactive gaming experiences. AI-driven non-player characters (NPCs) add depth and complexity to video games, making them more engaging. These NPCs can adapt to your actions, providing dynamic and unpredictable interactions. Adaptive learning algorithms adjust the game's difficulty level based on your skill, ensuring you are consistently challenged without feeling overwhelmed. This personalized gameplay keeps you engaged and enhances the overall gaming experience.

Thanks to AI, visual effects in film and television have also seen significant advancements. AI-powered motion capture technology allows for more realistic and fluid animations. Actors' movements are captured in real-time and translated into digital characters with incredible accuracy. AI tools for color correction and visual effects enable filmmakers to create stunning visuals, enhancing storytelling. These tools can automatically adjust lighting, add special effects, and even generate entire scenes, reducing the time and effort required for post-production.

Case Study: Imani's TikTok Reach Boosted by AI

Imani Brown, a content creator focusing on self-confidence and kindness for tweens and teenagers, initially struggled to grow her audience on TikTok. The crowded social media landscape made it hard to stand out. To overcome this, Imani turned to AI tools to enhance her content strategy and increase her reach. Specifically, AI analyzed her video performance and suggested the best times to post, ideal video lengths, and themes that resonated most with her audience. AI algorithms also helped Imani identify new audiences by analyzing similar accounts and recommending hashtags, trends, and collaborations to boost her visibility.

Additionally, AI-powered tools automated responses to comments and messages, allowing Imani to maintain timely interactions while focusing on high-engagement comments. AI also optimized her content distribution, disseminating her videos to users interested in similar topics and increasing her reach. Finally, AI provided feedback on how her content was perceived, allowing her to adjust her messaging to stay relevant and impactful.

By using AI, Imani grew her audience dramatically. Within a few months, her videos reached over a million tweens and teenagers, many of whom shared how her content positively impacted their confidence and resilience. AI expanded her reach and strengthened her connection with her followers, building a supportive community around her message.

PERSONALIZING LEARNING AND ACCELERATING RESEARCH

AI's transformative effects on education cannot be overstated. AI is creating personalized learning experiences tailored to student's unique needs. Imagine a classroom where each student receives customized lessons that adapt to their learning pace and style. Adaptive learning platforms, such as Khan Academy, use AI to analyze students' strengths and weaknesses, tailoring content to fill gaps in knowledge and challenge them appropriately. These platforms track progress in real-time, offering immediate feedback and adjusting the difficulty level accordingly.

Personalized tutoring systems take this a step further by providing one-on-one support. AI-powered tutors identify areas where students struggle, offering targeted explanations and practice problems. This individualized attention helps students grasp complex concepts more effectively than traditional methods.

Beyond the classroom, AI streamlines numerous administrative tasks in educational institutions, such as simplifying student enrollment and course scheduling, by analyzing data on course demand, student preferences, and faculty availability. This ensures courses are optimally scheduled, reducing conflicts and maximizing resource utilization.

Automated grading and assessment tools enhance efficiency by quickly evaluating assignments and exams. These tools use natural language processing to grade essays and provide feedback, saving educators time and allowing them to focus on more meaningful student interactions.

AI also plays a significant role in student support, providing timely and practical guidance. AI chatbots assist with academic advising and answer common questions about course requirements, deadlines, and campus resources. These chatbots are usually available all day, every day, offering students immediate support whenever needed. Predictive analytics identify at-risk students by analyzing academic performance, attendance, and engagement data. By flagging potential issues early on, educators can intervene with targeted support, helping students stay on track and succeed.

AI also accelerates educational research by analyzing vast datasets to uncover insights and trends. By processing and interpreting large volumes of academic papers to identify key findings and emerging topics, researchers are better able to stay updated with the latest developments and collaborate more effectively. AI also supports the development of new educational technologies, from intelligent tutoring systems to virtual reality learning environments, pushing the boundaries of what's possible in education.

Case Study: Aisha's AI-Enhanced Research in Behavioral Economics

Aisha Kumar, a PhD student in behavioral economics, explored how emotions, biases, and social influences shape economic decisions. Her research required vast amounts of data and complex analysis, prompting her to integrate AI tools into her methodology. Her AI-driven research involved:

- *Data Collection and Processing:* AI automated the gathering and cleaning of large datasets from surveys, transaction records, and social media, allowing Aisha to focus on analysis.
- *Pattern Recognition:* AI algorithms identified complex patterns, such as the influence of cognitive biases like

loss aversion on financial decisions, which traditional methods may have missed.
- *Predictive Modeling:* AI enabled Aisha to create models that simulated individual behavior under different conditions, incorporating psychological factors like stress and peer influence.
- *Natural Language Processing (NLP) for Qualitative Data:* AI's NLP analyzed interview and survey responses, extracting key themes and behavioral triggers, which Aisha cross-referenced with quantitative data.
- *Real-Time Adaptation:* AI tools allowed her to analyze data in real-time, adjusting her research approach to stay responsive to emerging patterns and events.

AI expanded the scope and depth of Aisha's study, revealing nuanced insights into economic behavior that traditional methods may have overlooked. Her predictive models and NLP-driven analysis became central to her thesis, showcasing how AI can bridge psychology and economics to understand human decision-making better.

IMPROVING WORKPLACE EFFICIENCY AND COLLABORATION

AI is making the workplace more efficient, productive, and collaborative. In hiring and employee onboarding, AI significantly streamlines recruitment processes. For example, when searching for candidates, AI can sift through hundreds of resumes in seconds, identifying those that match the job requirements based on keywords and skill sets. This automated search saves significant time and enables a more thorough review of applications than manual processes. Also, AI-driven systems provide new hires with personalized training programs during onboarding, helping them adapt to their new roles. These systems can answer common questions, schedule training sessions, and even offer virtual workplace tours, making the onboarding process smoother and more engaging.

From a productivity perspective, AI enhances both individual and team performance. AI tools help individuals manage time and tasks more effectively through AI-powered scheduling assistants that can organize meetings, set reminders, and prioritize tasks based on deadlines and importance. These tools free employees from administrative burdens, allowing them to focus on more critical tasks. For teams, AI facilitates better project management by tracking progress, predicting potential roadblocks, and suggesting solutions. Also, AI can analyze team performance data to identify strengths and weaknesses, enabling managers to allocate resources more efficiently and set realistic goals.

Collaboration and teamwork also benefit from AI's capabilities. AI team-building tools can suggest activities that encourage stronger interpersonal relationships based on team dynamics and individual preferences. In remote work environments, AI enhances collaboration by providing real-time translation services, ensuring language barriers do not impede communication. AI-driven platforms can also track project timelines, assign tasks, and facilitate virtual meetings, making remote collaboration as effective as in-person teamwork. For on-site collaboration, AI systems can analyze office layouts and suggest modifications to improve interaction and productivity, such as optimizing seating arrangements or identifying ideal spaces for collaboration zones.

AI's integration into the workplace illustrates its potential to revolutionize how we work, from hiring and onboarding to enhancing productivity and encouraging collaboration. This transformation makes operations more efficient and creates a more dynamic and engaging work environment.

Case Study: AI-Driven Collaboration and Innovation in Designing an Adaptive Lighting System for Clover City

An engineering team at a leading firm was tasked with designing an adaptive lighting system for Clover City. The system needed to adjust based on pedestrian movement, traffic flow, and environmental conditions while improving energy efficiency and safety. The project required collaboration across engineering disciplines, and the team integrated AI tools to enhance productivity and reduce costs.

The team used AI-powered platforms to streamline communication between software engineers, electrical engineers, and urban planners, ensuring real-time updates and reducing errors. AI simulations allowed the team to test the system under different conditions, predicting its functionality and energy efficiency. AI tools also provided design optimizations based on traffic patterns and environmental data, enabling quicker iterations. Real-time data integration from traffic cameras and sensors further enhanced decision-making, while predictive analytics helped avoid costly redesigns and kept the project within budget.

AI significantly improved collaboration and productivity, allowing the team to develop a highly efficient, adaptable lighting system for Clover City. The project was completed within budget and inspired other teams in the company to adopt AI-driven solutions for future urban infrastructure projects.

COFOUNDER TO INTERN: AI AND ENTREPRENEURSHIP

Artificial intelligence is reshaping the entrepreneurial landscape, offering tools and insights to sole proprietorships and small businesses that were once the domain of large corporations. One of the most profound changes is the ability of entrepreneurs to use AI to generate profitable business ideas. AI algorithms analyze market trends, consumer behavior, and emerging technologies to suggest viable business opportunities. This capability allows entrepreneurs to identify gaps in the market and develop innovative solutions. For instance, an AI tool might analyze social media trends to suggest a new product that caters to an emerging consumer need. In this regard, AI can be considered a business cofounder – a novel concept for many.

Starting a business involves numerous steps, and AI can provide specific guidance through each phase. AI-powered platforms offer actionable advice on business planning, from crafting a business model to securing funding. These platforms can generate logos and business names and even create websites tailored to your brand. It's like having a virtual intern that handles all the basics, allowing you to focus on the strategic side of your business. AI also excels in lead generation, identifying potential customers and partners by analyzing data from various sources. This targeted approach streamlines marketing efforts and boosts the chances of success.

Developing a product from scratch is a significant and often costly endeavor, but AI can simplify and shorten the process. AI tools assist in design, testing, and optimization from prototyping to final production. AI algorithms can, for instance, simulate different design models, identify flaws, and suggest improvements. This accelerates the development process, reducing time and costs. AI enhances business productivity once the product is ready by acting as a virtual intern, handling routine tasks such as data entry, scheduling, and customer support, freeing up your time to focus on strategic growth. Another area where AI shines is in decision-making. By analyzing a significant amount of data, AI provides insights that inform strategic choices, such as offering recommendations for pricing strategies, market expansion, or product diversification. Furthermore, AI enables scale-process automation, guaranteeing consistent quality and efficiency, from supply chain management to customer relationship management, making operations more streamlined and responsive.

No one said entrepreneurship is easy, and the financial ups and downs aren't for everyone. However, as we are learning, AI is a significant game changer for those with an entrepreneurial spirit; anyone can get into the 'game' because of AI. For example, AI enables non-engineers to innovate in new ways, meaning you don't need a technical background to develop new products or create launch plans, opening incredible opportunities that may once have felt out of reach. However, as AI becomes more accessible globally, competition will intensify, making it vital to innovate and adapt continually.

Utilizing readily available AI tools means you don't always have to build proprietary technologies, saving you significant time and money, both of which can be in short supply when starting a business. Content creation tasks, such as writing company policies and training manuals, can be 'outsourced' to AI, allowing you to concentrate on revenue-generating activities. AI also generates instant feedback, helping entrepreneurs quickly assess the viability of ideas and products. This real-time analysis optimizes marketing and advertising efforts, ensuring your campaigns are effective. However, entrepreneurs must also beware of bias in AI algorithms, which can skew results and lead to suboptimal decisions. Regulatory changes may also impact how AI can be used, so entrepreneurs must stay informed about legal developments.

While AI can do many things, supporting entrepreneurs from concept ideation to business planning to product development to sales and marketing, it is important to remember that *humans still matter*. While AI offers powerful tools, human creativity, empathy, and judgment remain irreplaceable.

Case Study: Launching Samantha's Sustainable Skincare Business

Samantha Lee, an aspiring entrepreneur passionate about sustainability, wanted to start a zero-waste skincare line. As a first-time business owner, she used AI tools to guide her through launching and growing her business. The AI-driven success of her business involved:

- *Business Idea Generation:* AI suggested several business concepts based on Samantha's interest in eco-friendly skincare and market trends. She chose to create a line of zero-waste, organic skincare products that aligned with her values and growing consumer demand.
- *Business Setup:* AI guided Samantha step-by-step through registering her business, obtaining permits, and finding sustainable packaging and ingredients suppliers.

- *Market Research and Strategy:* AI conducted thorough market research, helping Samantha understand consumer behaviors and competitor strategies. It also developed a marketing strategy targeting her key demographic with a focus on sustainability.
- *Task Automation:* AI handled mundane tasks, allowing Samantha to focus on product development and growth.
- *Feedback and Adaptation:* After launching, AI provided real-time feedback on marketing, sales, and customer satisfaction, allowing Samantha to adapt quickly and optimize her product offerings.

With AI's help, Samantha successfully launched her zero-waste skincare line, and her products sold out within weeks. The AI-generated business idea, targeted marketing, and streamlined operations gave her a competitive edge. Her business thrives, with plans to expand into new markets supported by ongoing AI insights.

PROTECTING THE PUBLIC WITH AI

Regulators are essential to protecting the public interest. They do this by establishing standards for professions, including physicians and surgeons, engineers, nurses, dentists, and more, ensuring that practitioners meet specific competencies needed for their practice and conduct their practice ethically and in accordance with the legislation that governs them. Regulators oversee everything from medical licenses to real estate certifications, maintaining the integrity and trustworthiness of various fields. By setting entry-to-practice standards, they ensure that only qualified individuals can offer services to the public, protecting consumers and patients from incompetence and malpractice.

AI can enhance entry-to-practice standards. Again, by analyzing vast amounts of data from exams, training programs, and field performance, regulators ensure that the standards are stringent, fair, and representative of best practices. This data-driven approach allows for continuous improvement of the qualification process by, for example, identifying trends in examination performance to adjust the difficulty level, ensuring that the tests accurately reflect the skills needed in the profession.

When filing complaints against professionals, AI provides a streamlined process for the public. Automated systems can guide individuals through the complaint submission process, ensuring all necessary information is collected.

Regulators can benefit significantly from AI in overseeing the complaints and discipline processes. For example, AI systems can track the progress of each complaint, ensuring that none slip through the cracks. These systems can prioritize cases based on severity and complexity, allocating resources more effectively and helping to reduce backlog. During investigations, AI assists by cross-referencing various data sources, such as previous complaints, professional records, and even public databases, to build a comprehensive case. This thorough approach not only speeds up the investigation process but also increases the accuracy and fairness of the outcomes.

AI streamlines administrative tasks, too. For regulators, this means automating routine tasks such as scheduling inspections, renewing licenses, and updating records, freeing staff to focus on more critical issues. Furthermore, AI can predict when certain licenses are due for renewal and send automated reminders, ensuring compliance and reducing the administrative burden on regulators and the professionals they regulate.

To maximize the benefits of AI while mitigating risks, regulators must establish clear policies regarding its use. These policies should address data privacy and security to protect sensitive information. They should also ensure transparency in how AI algorithms make decisions, providing explanations that regulated professionals and the public can understand. Additionally, policies must include measures to detect and correct any biases within AI systems, ensuring that all disciplinary actions are fair and just. By considering these factors, regulators can harness the power of AI to enhance their effectiveness while maintaining public trust.

Case Study: AI-Driven Bias Detection in the Regulation of Dental Professionals

The Dental Regulatory Authority (DRA) oversees dental practice in Pennsylvania, ensuring that licensed dental professionals adhere to the highest standards of care and ethics. The DRA reviews patient complaints and takes disciplinary actions when necessary.

Concerned about increased complaints against dentists from specific ethnic backgrounds, the DRA integrated AI tools into its complaint review process to detect potential bias.

The AI system analyzed thousands of complaints, identifying patterns such as disproportionate targeting of certain groups. Using advanced detection algorithms, it flagged complaints with implicit or explicit bias and assigned a bias score to inform the DRA's decisions.

Based on these findings, the DRA implemented training programs to raise staff awareness of unconscious bias and revised its review process to include AI-generated bias assessments as a mandatory step. The AI system continuously monitored new complaints, allowing for real-time adjustments to strategies and training.

This AI integration helped the DRA detect and mitigate bias, ensuring fair treatment of all dental professionals and enhancing trust in the regulatory process. The AI-driven approach set a new standard for promoting fairness in professional oversight.

APPLYING AI SKILLS IN YOUR CURRENT JOB

Identifying opportunities for AI integration in your current job can significantly enhance your efficiency and effectiveness. For most of us, leveraging AI in some way is no longer optional if we want to remain competitive. One recent survey by Ernst and Young suggests more than 90% of people use AI at work. Most see the value in adopting AI in the workplace because they believe it will make them more efficient and productive and enable them to focus on higher-value tasks. You can integrate AI into your work by analyzing your workflows to pinpoint areas where AI can optimize processes. For example, if your role involves repetitive tasks like data entry or scheduling, consider an AI-driven solution that can automate these tasks, enabling you to focus on more strategic activities.*

Collaboration is crucial when implementing AI solutions. Working closely with data scientists and AI engineers can close the divide between technical and non-technical teams. It's essential to communicate AI concepts in a way everyone can understand, ensuring all team members see AI projects' value and potential impact. This cross-functional collaboration encourages a more inclusive environment, improving idea-sharing and solution development. Involving diverse perspectives enables the creation of more robust and effective AI implementations tailored to your organizational needs.

Demonstrating the impact of AI projects is vital for gaining support and securing further investment. Use key performance indicators to measure the effectiveness of AI initiatives. These metrics could include time saved, error reduction, or increased productivity. Presenting these results to management and other stakeholders through detailed case studies and clear, concise reports can showcase the tangible benefits of AI. Highlighting real-world examples of success can build organizational confidence in AI's potential and encourage broader adoption.

Finally, continuous improvement is at the heart of effective AI integration. Therefore, regularly iterate on your AI projects, using feedback and new data to refine and enhance the solutions and stay updated with AI trends and tools to maintain a competitive edge.

---

* For security reasons, be sure any tools or platforms you use at work are approved by your company's IT department, especially if you're working with secure information.

EVERYDAY AI

Alexa, Siri, and Google Assistant have become household names, changing how we interact with technology. Advanced AI algorithms enable voice recognition and natural language processing, allowing these virtual assistants to set timers or play your favorite song on command. The technology behind these assistants involves machine learning models trained on vast datasets of spoken language, allowing them to understand various accents, dialects, and even contextual nuances. This seamless interaction makes it feel like you are conversing with a knowledgeable companion!

AI's influence extends beyond virtual assistants into home automation, creating more connected living spaces. Thermostats, like Nest, use AI to learn your heating and cooling preferences, adjusting the temperature automatically to maintain comfort while optimizing energy usage. AI-powered home security systems enhance safety by using facial recognition to identify family members and alert you to any unfamiliar faces. These systems can also distinguish between everyday activities and potential threats, reducing false alarms and providing peace of mind. AI can even be integrated into home systems to control appliances, including gas stoves.

AI also significantly benefits personal productivity, streamlining daily tasks and improving efficiency. Personal finance management apps like Empower Personal Dashboard and YNAB (You Need A Budget) use AI to track spending habits, help you set goals, categorize expenses, and offer budgeting advice, as in the earlier case study about Mark using AI to optimize his finances.

AI-powered email filtering and scheduling tools, like Google's Smart Compose and Calendar, save you time by suggesting email responses and optimizing your appointments. These tools learn from your behavior and make personalized suggestions that enhance productivity and simplify task management. Even your hobbies and interests benefit from AI. If you're into fitness, wearable devices like Garmin Fenix, Apple Watch, and Oura Ring use AI to monitor physical activity, analyze workout patterns, and provide personalized exercise plans, offering real-time feedback and motivation, helping you achieve your fitness goals. If you enjoy cooking, AI-powered recipe recommendation systems, like those in connected fridges or apps like Yummly, suggest meal plans based on your dietary preferences and the ingredients you currently have available. These systems can even guide you through cooking steps, making meal preparation more enjoyable and efficient.

* * *

CHAPTER 2 SELF-ASSESSMENT

Feeling confident about what you've learned? Put your knowledge to the test with a brief ten-question quiz. Just scan the QR code below or enter this link into your browser [**https://tinyurl.com/AICh2Quiz**] for a quick, engaging review that'll take only a few minutes.

QR code for the Chapter 2 quiz.

THREE
HANDS-ON EXPLORATION OF AI

Now, it's time to roll up your sleeves! This chapter will introduce you to some of the most important tools you'll need as you venture further into your exploration of AI.

From writing your first lines of code to creating several functioning applications, you'll gain practical skills that can be applied in multiple real-world contexts.

While you won't be a computer programmer or data scientist after completing the exercises in this chapter, they are designed to be educational and enjoyable. They will hopefully whet your appetite to learn more and give you the confidence to tackle more complex AI challenges.

GETTING STARTED WITH AI TOOLS

Becoming acquainted with fundamental AI tools and platforms that will assist you every step of the way as you embark on your AI learning journey is crucial. Enter Python, a programming language notable for its straightforward syntax and readability. Python is at the heart of AI development. Experts use it, but it is especially beneficial for beginners, as complex AI concepts are more accessible. Python is strengthened by an extensive array of libraries and frameworks precisely engineered for AI tasks, offering a robust toolkit at your disposal.

What are Python libraries?

Python libraries extend Python's capabilities. They are collections of pre-written code and functions that make it easier for developers to work on specific tasks. Essentially, they prevent developers from starting from scratch or reinventing the wheel. Libraries are typically built by developers and run by a community of volunteers who make them freely available to the public. The term open-source software describes such products because of their accessibility and the collaborative nature in which they are built and run.

In this chapter, you will be introduced to several Python libraries, including TensorFlow. TensorFlow is an open-source machine learning framework crucial to AI development. This library equips developers with the capability to construct and train neural networks. Neural networks empower your projects to learn from datasets and progressively adapt and enhance their performance. (For a refresher on neural networks, revisit Chapter 1.)

Another Python library we will explore is scikit-learn. Scikit-learn simplifies data mining and analysis. It is known for being a straightforward and effective tool widely used by developers. Scikit-learn is crucial for crafting machine learning models as it provides a comprehensive suite of algorithms, making it a flexible choice for many AI applications.

Effectively using these libraries requires having a conducive development environment that enables you to write and implement your code seamlessly. One such development environment is Jupyter Notebooks, an interactive coding platform that lets you compartmentalize your code into manageable blocks, offering immediate feedback on code execution, like letting you know if there's a mistake in your code and what and where it is. It also enables you to annotate your coding process as you go. These features render

Jupyter Notebooks an excellent environment for learning and experimenting with AI concepts.

While Python, Jupyter Notebooks, and other libraries and tools can be downloaded onto your computer, we will undertake the activities in this chapter on the Google Colab platform.* This hosted Jupyter Notebook service requires no setup. Of course, should you wish to download the latest version of Python on your computer, you can do so on the official Python website [**www.python.org**]. Still, I need to stress this is unnecessary as beginners and experts alike regularly use cloud-based platforms such as Google Colab to undertake their projects. Colab allows you to write and execute Python code directly in your browser without requiring installation. Also, many popular Python libraries, such as TensorFlow, scikit-learn, and more, have been preinstalled, making it ideal for your future needs and the activities you will undertake in this chapter.

Google Colab is free to use. While you don't need a Google Account to access Colab, having one is highly recommended for several reasons. First, with a Google Account, your notebooks will be saved on your personal Google Drive, making them easy to access, update, and tweak whenever you wish and from wherever you are. Second, you can easily share your notebooks, allowing for collaboration. Third, when you're signed in to your Google Account, your Colab session will last longer, enabling you to work for more extended periods. Finally, some features like saving and exporting notebooks are only available when you're signed into your Google Account.

To access Google Colab, type "Google Colab" in your browser; it should be the first search result. You can also go directly to Google Colab's website [**https://colab.research.google.com/**].

We will begin with the Python basics as we progress through this chapter. The first three projects you'll undertake include a simple

---

* There are many other platforms for people looking to learn Python. For example, Anaconda [**https://www.anaconda.com/**] is widely recognized as a top-tier platform and is also free. Anaconda has teamed up with Microsoft to introduce Python into Excel, providing unparalleled data analysis capabilities.

calculator program, a to-do list application, and a trivia game. These initial projects are designed to introduce you to core programming concepts in an applied manner.

We will then explore TensorFlow by constructing a basic neural network. In this exercise, you'll gain practical experience training your network with sample data and evaluating its effectiveness, which will deepen your understanding of machine learning model dynamics.

Next, we'll harness the scikit-learn library to build an image classification model. This project involves loading a dataset, preparing the data for processing, and training a decision tree classifier. We'll investigate methodologies for assessing the model's performance to ensure your classifier is accurate and reliable.

Concluding this section, we will venture into Natural Language Processing (NLP) utilizing NLTK (Natural Language Toolkit), a platform for building Python models that utilize natural (human) language data. We will use NLTK to create a sentiment analysis tool.

After these tutorials, you will have a solid appreciation for AI development and will have started to build a portfolio of AI projects. I hope you'll be confident in taking on more sophisticated projects over time. The tools and know-how you acquire here will help form a robust foundation for your continuous learning and innovation in the AI domain.

PYTHON BASICS

Python is one of the preferred computer programming languages for AI development due to its simplicity and readability. Other commonly used programming languages include C++, Java, and R, but in this book, we will stick with Python as it tops the list. Python is great for learning programming as it's clear and straightforward. For instance, Python boasts easy-to-read syntax, allowing you to focus on understanding AI concepts rather than getting mired in complex code. As we learned earlier, its extensive libraries and frameworks specifically designed for AI, such as TensorFlow, scikit-learn, and NLTK, make it a potent tool.

Additionally, Python is supported by a sizable and vibrant user base that offers a wealth of guides, discussion boards, and other tools to aid in learning and problem-solving.

Python's basic syntax is designed to be intuitive. Variables in Python do not require explicit declarations, making it easy to define them as needed. For example, x = 5 assigns the value 5 to the variable x. Python supports various data types, including integers, floats, strings, and lists. Operators like +, -, *, and / allow you to perform arithmetic operations.

Before we proceed, let's explore floats, strings, and lists in Python. A float is a function or reusable code that converts values into floating-point numbers, which are decimal or fractional numbers such as 33.56, 3000.45, or 10897.56.

A string is a sequence of characters presented in single or double quotes, such as "name," which contains a sequence of characters 'n', 'a', 'm', 'e'.

A list is like a collection of things enclosed in square brackets, with each thing separated by a comma. A list of numbers might look like this: List = [18, 36, 54].

Control structures in Python, such as for loops and conditionals, are straightforward. A for loop iterates over a sequence (like a list, string, range, or tuple), while conditional if statements execute code based on specified conditions. Such functions in Python are defined using the def keyword, followed by the function name and parameters.

As you work through the activities in this book, you'll be introduced to various Python syntax and coding concepts. While this book is not intended to teach Python programming in depth, it provides hands-on experience with Python code to give you a taste of what's possible. The goal is to whet your appetite for learning more. If you're ever curious about how a particular line of code works or want to dive deeper into the Python syntax you'll be working with, ChatGPT [**www.chatgpt.com**] is a great resource to help guide you through and deepen your understanding.

HANDS-ON ACTIVITIES USING PYTHON

A quick note: all step-by-step tutorials included in this book, including the three Python projects you'll be introduced to in this section, can be accessed by scanning the following QR code or typing **[https://tinyurl.com/AIHandsOnActivities]** into your internet browser.

QR code to access the hands-on activities.

Python Project #1: Creating a simple calculator program

This project involves designing a simple application that prompts users to select an arithmetic operation (addition, subtraction, multiplication, or division) and input two numerical values. Upon receiving the inputs, the program calculates and displays the result. This activity introduces you to some of Python's most straightforward syntax while reinforcing your understanding of variables and basic data types. It also introduces you to input and conditional statements. To access the step-by-step tutorial, including the Python code you'll need to build your calculator, either scan the QR code at the beginning of this section, or enter **[https://tinyurl.com/AIHandsOnActivities]** into your browser.

Python Project #2: Developing a to-do list application

This project is an excellent introduction to more complex Python concepts, such as lists for storing tasks, loops for iterating through tasks, and file operations for saving your to-do list so it persists between program runs. Through this exercise, you'll gain hands-on experience managing data collections and interfacing with the file system—a crucial skill set for any aspiring AI developer. The step-by-step tutorial, including the Python code you'll need to build your to-do list application can be accessed by scanning the QR code at the beginning of this section or entering [**https://tinyurl.com/AIHandsOnActivities**] into your browser.

Python Project #3: Creating a trivia game

This activity is an important and valuable part of your AI journey for several reasons. First, it reinforces basic Python skills, such as working with and defining functions, and introduces you to classes and control flow, which are crucial for anyone learning AI. Second, working with Python libraries is vital, so this activity introduces you to other Python libraries and demonstrates how to import them into your application. Third, it introduces you to event-driven programming, like handling button clicks, necessary for more complex AI concepts such as interactive AI features or real-time data processing. Fourth, you will gain experience creating a simple graphical user interface (GUI) that shows the practical side of AI, where AI models might be integrated into user-facing applications, like deploying an AI-powered chatbot. Also, let's face it: working on a visual and interactive project is engaging and motivating, which is necessary for maintaining interest in a topic like this! Fifth, this activity introduces you to data handling through a question-and-answer structure, another critical aspect of AI. Finally, this activity is flexible, enabling you to build on it as you progress along your journey, eventually expanding it into an AI-powered game that adapts questions based on the user's performance. With these points in mind, the QR code at the top of this section will take you to the step-by-step tutorial, or you can enter [**https://tinyurl.com/ AIHandsOnActivities**] into your browser.

THE IMPORTANCE OF VERSION CONTROL

Just as you'd want to save different versions of a report you're writing to keep records of the initial, subsequent, and final drafts, implementing version control is crucial for effective code management, particularly as your projects escalate in complexity.

Git, alongside GitHub, serves as the cornerstone for version control. It facilitates code change tracking and enables rollback to previous states as necessary. GitHub further enhances this by providing a collaborative environment for sharing and reviewing code.

GitHub is a web-based platform for version control and collaboration on software development projects. It's built on top of Git, a version control system that tracks changes to the file over time. Git and GitHub work with Google Colab and other development environments, including Python's built-in Integrated Development and Learning Environment (IDLE), which comes with the standard Python installation and is primarily used on local machines.

Using GitHub with Google Colab helps you manage and version-control programs and applications you work on, including the practice activities you've been undertaking. There are a few steps to take to integrate GitHub and Google Colab.

Using GitHub with Google Colab

First, go to GitHub [**https://github.com/**] and create an account if you don't already have one. Then, create a new repository:

- Click on the "+" icon in the top right corner and select "New Repository."

- Name your repository. For instance, you could call it "Trivia Game" for the project you just undertook. You also have the option to add a description if you like.
- Choose the repository visibility. It can be made public or kept private.
- Click "Create repository."

Second, open Google Colab and the notebook you want to connect with GitHub. I recommend connecting GitHub to your Trivia Game and then recreating the steps above for your other projects. To sign in to GitHub from Google Colab, click on "File" > "Save a copy in GitHub…". You may be prompted to sign into GitHub and authorize Google Colab to access your GitHub account. Once you've signed in, select the repository you created ("Trivia Game").

Third, after you've selected the repository and named your file, click "OK" to save your notebook directly to GitHub. This will create a new file in your GitHub repository with the current state of your Colab notebook. Each time you make changes in Google Colab and want to save them to GitHub, go to "File" > "Save a copy in GitHub…" You can add a commit message to describe the changes. For instance, using the Trivia Game as an example, you can save the first version you created to the repository, and then after adding in more advanced features, such as an enhanced Graphical User Interface (GUI), you can save it again with a commit message like "Improved the GUI by adding a progress bar and bolding questions for additional visibility."

To access notebooks from GitHub in Google Colab, click on "File" > "Open notebook," select the "GitHub" tab (you may need to sign in and authorize access again), enter your GitHub repository's name in the search bar, and select the notebook you want to open. Then you can make edits to the notebook in Google Colab and save your changes back to GitHub by going to "File" > "Save a copy in GitHub…" You can also view the version history by clicking "History" to see all the changes you made to the notebook. Further, you can work with others on the notebook by adding them as collaborators in the repository settings, allowing them to clone the repository, make changes, and submit pull requests, a method used in GitHub to notify collaborators that you've completed some work that you want to merge into the main file.

Practical Steps: Create repositories for your Python projects

Try creating a repository for activities 1, 2, and 3 to practice these steps. Then, when you make changes to any of these programs and applications in the future, you can save your notebooks to GitHub after each session, adding commit messages to track progress. To take this a step further, if you know someone more advanced than you in Python, try adding them as a collaborator and work with them to add new enhancements or features. This collaboration feature is an excellent way to learn and build out applications and programs faster. Since all of this is on the cloud, remember that you can access and continue your work from any device, anywhere, by opening the notebook directly from GitHub in Google Colab.

* * *

FIRST STEPS WITH TENSORFLOW

TensorFlow is a powerful tool widely recognized for its versatility and performance, like the Swiss Army knife of the AI world. It's an open-source machine learning framework enabling you to build and train neural networks. TensorFlow is indispensable for a wide range of tasks. For example, if you're trying to teach a computer to recognize your cat in photos or understand human speech, TensorFlow is the right tool. Like Python, TensorFlow benefits from having a large community of users behind it, from new-to-AI users to advanced AI wizards. Let's give TensorFlow a try by creating a simple neural network.

TensorFlow Project: Building a simple neural network to recognize handwritten digits

This exercise aims to train a neural network to recognize handwritten digits (0-9) using the MNIST (Modified National Institute of Standards and Technology) dataset. The MNIST dataset contains 70,000 images of handwritten digits divided into training and test sets; the former includes 60,000 images, and the latter contains 10,000. Each image in the dataset is a 28x28 pixel greyscale image (784 pixels in total), with each pixel ranging from 0 (black) to 255 (white) with various shades of grey in between. Think of this as the "content" of each image. The images in the dataset are labeled with the correct digit they represent, so the task is to train a model to correctly classify these images based on their content.

Scanning the QR code below or entering [**https://tinyurl.com/AIHandsOnActivities**] into your browser will take you to the step-by-step tutorial for this activity.

QR code to access the hands-on activities.

BUILDING SIMPLE MODELS WITH SCIKIT-LEARN

Scikit-learn is a leading Python library tailored for machine learning. It stands out for its beginner-friendly design. Its straightforward and efficient framework simplifies the learning curve, making it an ideal data mining and analysis environment. With scikit-learn, you can access an extensive suite of tools for crafting machine learning models, encompassing various approaches such as classification, regression, and clustering.

The library's user-centered interface simplifies the complexity of syntax, allowing you to concentrate on grasping the concepts and refining your skills through hands-on experimentation.

Scikit-learn Project: Building a decision tree classification model

In this activity, we will construct a simple decision tree classification model, a practical starting point for utilizing scikit-learn. This activity reinforces the machine learning basics we've begun learning in the previous exercises, including model training and evaluation. It will also give you hands-on experience with some core steps in building a simple machine-learning model.

For this endeavor, we will use the iris dataset, a classic dataset often used when teaching machine learning. It contains measurements of different parts of the iris flower, like petal and sepal length and width, and the flower species, such as the Setosa, Virginica, and Versicolor irises. The model aims to predict an iris species based on measurements.

The instructions to complete this activity can be accessed via the QR code below, or by entering [**https://tinyurl.com/AIHandsOnActivities**] into your internet browser.

QR code to access the hands-on activities.

HANDS-ON EXPLORATION OF AI

After running the model, it will produce several outputs, including a classification report.

Classification Report:

	precision	recall	f1-score	support
setosa	1.00	1.00	1.00	10
versicolor	1.00	1.00	1.00	9
virginica	1.00	1.00	1.00	11
accuracy			1.00	30
macro avg	1.00	1.00	1.00	30
weighted avg	1.00	1.00	1.00	30

> *Reproduction of the classification report provided as an output by the decision tree classification model using the iris dataset.*

Consider this illustrative example to help you understand this report. You're a botanist specializing in iris flowers and have created a clever tool to identify different iris species in gardens and mixed bouquets. You want to test this tool on your research garden to see how well it performs. The results come in a special report card called a classification report, like a detailed flower journal, telling you about the "precision," "recall," "F1-score," and "support" for each iris species (Setosa, Versicolor, and Virginica). "Precision" is how often your tool correctly identifies each iris type. For instance, when it says, "This is a Setosa," how frequently is it right?

On the other hand, "recall" shows how good your tool is at finding all the Setosas in the garden. Did it spot every single one, or did some Setosas go unnoticed? The "F1-score" cleverly balances these two aspects. It's like asking, "Is the tool good at spotting Setosas and not mistaking other irises for Setosas?" It combines precision and recall into one measure.

"Support" counts how many of each iris type you tested. This is important because it tells you if you have a fair representation of each species in your garden.

The classification report shows that your iris-identifying tool did amazingly well, correctly naming every single iris! While this sounds wonderful, it's not necessarily ideal, as this perfect score could mean the tool is "overfitting," which is like memorizing every detail about the irises in your research garden down to the tiniest vein on a petal. That's great for identifying those exact flowers but might lead to struggles when seeing a new iris that looks similar but not identical.

To avoid this, we can try a few strategies. We could stop our tool's training early before it starts memorizing too many specifics. Or we could give it less time to study each iris. Another option is to show a wider variety of irises during training.

However, the iris dataset we're using in our classification model is famously small. Therefore, our best approach might be simplifying our tool's method to prevent the model from overfitting. If we use a decision tree, we could make it shallower. For example, instead of asking specific questions like "Is the sepal exactly 5.1 cm long?" we stick to broader questions like "Are the sepals long or short?" This straightforward approach might miss some finer details, but it's often better at handling new, slightly different irises. It's the difference between memorizing exact quiz answers about irises and grasping the underlying concepts of iris biology. We aim to create an iris-identifying tool that can confidently classify irises in any garden or bouquet, not just the one it was trained on!

USING NLTK FOR SENTIMENT ANALYSIS

Sentiment analysis helps organizations and individuals understand emotions and opinions expressed in text data, such as social media posts, product reviews, news articles, and more. Before AI, sentiment analysis was conducted by human reviewers who would read through texts and manually categorize them as positive, negative, or neutral. This was highly laborious, time-consuming, and prone to human error and bias. The limitations imposed by manual and other rule-based sentiment analysis led to the development and adoption of AI-based methods that are more accurate, scalable, efficient, and capable of understanding the complexities of human language. While not perfect and potentially subject to bias, AI-driven sentiment analysis is used in many crucial ways, including tracking brand reputation, monitoring customer satisfaction, detecting emerging trends and potential crises, and more. Sentiment analysis is valuable in many fields, including marketing, tourism and hospitality, finance, politics, human resources, and education.

Natural Language Toolkit (NLTK) Project: Building a sentiment analysis tool

This tool harnesses the power of Natural Language Processing (NLP) to evaluate the emotional tone behind textual data using the movie review dataset from NLTK. The tool can classify text into positive or negative sentiments by analyzing thousands of movie reviews. The dataset you'll download from NLTK contains a balanced collection of 2,000 movie reviews, half positive and the other half negative, allowing the tool to learn from a wide range of opinions and emotions real users express.

The sentiment analysis model is built using machine learning algorithms trained to detect language patterns—words, phrases, and punctuation—allowing it to recognize the difference between praise and criticism. As it processes new reviews, the model can identify key indicators of sentiment, such as adjectives, verbs, and subtle nuances in tone and context, allowing it to accurately predict whether a review is favorable or unfavorable.

The tool's power lies in its ability to analyze the richness of human language. It recognizes that sentiment is not just about individual words but how they're used together to convey a mood, opinion, or emotional response. Whether it's a brief critique or a lengthy recommendation, the tool captures the underlying sentiment of each review, providing users with meaningful insights.

Try your hand at building a sentiment analysis tool. Scan the QR code to access the step-by-step tutorial, or enter [**https://tinyurl.com/AIHandsOnActivities**] into your browser.

QR code to access the hands-on activities.

* * *

CHAPTER 3 SELF-ASSESSMENT

Ensure you've got everything down pat by taking a moment to tackle the post-chapter multiple-choice quiz! Scan the QR code or enter [**https://tinyurl.com/AICh3Quiz**] into your browser.

QR code to access the Chapter 3 quiz.

FOUR
ETHICAL AI

You're not alone if you're anxious about AI's dizzying rise in nearly all aspects of our lives. AI anxiety is real; it's logical for us to feel this way about this technology, especially when headlines suggest AI is more intelligent than us, produces better content, is more innovative, and is set to replace us all at work. I assure you that I had similar feelings when I began my journey with AI. However, the more I've used AI and engaged in this topic, the more I recognize how much humans matter and that good work is being done to ensure AI's ethical and responsible use.

We've covered many of AI's benefits thus far, noting how incredibly powerful and helpful this technology can be in many contexts, such as Gayle's early cancer diagnosis and Mark's financial optimization. Now, it's important we explore a range of ethical considerations in AI to have a balanced view of this technology.

Recall our earlier discussion on how AI is transforming the financial sector. We learned that AI systems can make crucial decisions about your eligibility for a loan in milliseconds by examining various factors, from your cell phone and social media usage to your transaction history, credit score, and more. These AI-driven decisions can profoundly impact your life. So, what happens if the AI system is biased or lacks transparency? This is where the importance of ethical AI comes into play.

Ethical AI involves developing and using AI systems that align with societal values, human rights, ethics, and moral principles to ensure that AI technologies are designed and deployed responsibly and safeguard against potential harms that could arise from their misuse.

The practice of ethical AI is crucial because it directly impacts our societal framework. Aligning AI development with societal values means ensuring these systems respect human dignity, fairness, and justice. When AI systems are used in healthcare to diagnose diseases or recommend treatments, for example, they must do so without discriminating against any group of patients. This alignment ensures that AI serves the greater good, enhancing human well-being rather than undermining it.

When ethical considerations in AI are ignored, severe consequences arise. One significant risk is the violation of privacy and individual rights. Large volumes of personal data are needed for AI systems to operate efficiently. If this data is mishandled, it can lead to privacy breaches, exposing sensitive information to unauthorized parties. Additionally, unethical AI can reinforce existing biases and inequalities. For instance, if an AI system used in hiring is trained on biased data, it may perpetuate discriminatory practices, favoring specific demographics over others. That AI can enable the spread of false information is another serious concern. Deepfakes—AI-generated fake videos or audio recordings that are difficult to separate from reality—can spread false information, undermining trust in media and creating social discord.

To counter these risks, several principles should guide the development and deployment of AI. In 2023, the United Nations leadership endorsed ten principles for the ethical use of AI, developed by the Inter-Agency Working Group on AI chaired by the International Telecommunication Union (ITU) and the United Nations Educational, Scientific and Cultural Organization (UNESCO).

Ten principles of ethical AI

1. *Avoid Harm:* AI should not cause harm to individuals, society, or the environment.
2. *Clear Purpose:* AI should have a clear and justified use without exceeding its intended scope.
3. *Safety First:* Reduce risks throughout the AI's life to protect people and the environment.
4. *Fair Treatment:* Ensure AI systems are fair, unbiased, and equitably distribute risks and benefits.
5. *Long-Term Thinking:* AI use should promote sustainable well-being for the future.
6. *Protect Privacy:* Respect and safeguard individuals' privacy rights.
7. *Human Control:* Humans must remain in charge of AI decisions.
8. *Clear Communication:* Be transparent about AI's decisions and explain them clearly.
9. *Take Responsibility:* Implement systems to monitor and ensure responsible AI use.
10. *Inclusion:* Engage all relevant stakeholders in AI design and usage.

The UN's ten principles for the ethical use of AI is one of several frameworks. Google, for example, also has a set of AI principles that guide the company's responsible AI research and development. There are other initiatives aimed at encouraging the ethical use of AI, such as AI for Good, an ongoing webinar series organized by ITU that brings together AI innovators and problem owners (those affected by the issue and would benefit from the solution) to connect, learn, and discuss AI solutions to solve global challenges such as poverty alleviation, improvements in health outcomes, and access to education.

PRIVACY CONCERNS

Protecting user data is paramount in our data-driven world, especially AI applications. Personal data forms the backbone of many AI models, enabling them to learn and make predictions. When you interact with an AI-powered service, whether a personalized shopping recommendation or a virtual assistant, your data is analyzed to enhance the service's accuracy and relevance. However, this reliance on personal data brings significant risks. Data breaches can expose sensitive information, leading to identity theft, financial loss, and erosion of trust. Misuse of data can result in unauthorized surveillance, discrimination, and other unethical practices, underscoring the need for stringent data privacy measures.

Ensuring data privacy in AI applications involves several robust techniques, including data anonymization, pseudonymization, and differential privacy. Data anonymization is a process where personally identifiable information is removed or modified, making it impossible to trace data back to an individual. Pseudonymization goes further by replacing private identifiers with fake identifiers or pseudonyms. These techniques protect user identity while retaining the data's utility for analysis. Differential privacy is another advanced method that introduces random noise into the data, ensuring individual privacy while allowing accurate data analysis. This technique balances the need for data privacy with the requirement for high-quality AI models.

Regulations and legal frameworks are essential for protecting data privacy. One of the world's toughest privacy and security laws is Europe's General Data Protection Regulation (GDPR). By requiring express consent for data collection and allowing people to view and remove their data, it establishes a high standard for data protection. This law applies to organizations worldwide that target or gather information about individuals residing in the European Union.

The California Consumer Privacy Act (CCPA) offers similar protections. This landmark U.S. law grants California consumers six key privacy rights: the right to know what personal data is collected and how it's used, the right to delete it, the right to opt out of its sale or sharing, the right to correct inaccuracies, and the right to limit its use. It also ensures individuals are not discriminated against for exercising these rights.

The AI Act in the European Union is the first comprehensive AI regulation in the world. The EU parliament adopted the AI Act in March 2024, and the Council of the EU gave its final approval two months later, in May 2024. The AI Act includes rules for different risk levels. An AI system considered a threat to people will be banned, such as systems that manipulate the cognitive behavior of people or vulnerable groups like children, systems that deploy a form of social scoring like classifying people based on their characteristics or socio-economic status, and systems that use real-time and remote biometric identification systems such as facial recognition. The Act also includes several transparency requirements, such as disclosing AI-generated content. In addition, the Act supports safe innovation by offering start-ups and small and medium-sized organizations the opportunity to develop and train AI models in a testing environment simulating real-world conditions before their release to the public. Such laws protect individuals and establish a level playing field for businesses, nurturing trust and accountability in AI technologies.

Developers must adopt best practices to maintain data privacy in their AI projects. Implementing robust data encryption ensures data is securely stored and transmitted, making it inaccessible to unauthorized parties. Regular privacy impact assessments help identify potential risks and vulnerabilities in AI systems, allowing developers to address them proactively. These assessments evaluate how data is collected, stored, and used, ensuring compliance with legal standards and ethical principles. By following these practices, developers can build AI systems that respect user privacy, promoting user trust and confidence.

* * *

AVOIDING BIAS

Bias in AI models refers to systematic errors that lead to unfair outcomes, affecting individuals or groups disproportionately. For example, if an AI system designed to screen job applications exhibits bias, it might unfairly favor applicants of a particular gender, race, or background, leading to unequal opportunities. This bias can have serious consequences, perpetuating societal prejudices and reinforcing inequalities. Racial bias in facial recognition systems has been well-documented, where these systems are less accurate in identifying individuals with darker skin tones. This can lead to wrongful accusations or even arrests, highlighting the critical need to address bias in AI.

As serious as bias in AI is, consider this perspective:

> "There is a silver lining on [sic] the bias issue. For example, say you have an algorithm trying to predict who should get a promotion. And say there was a supermarket chain that, statistically speaking, didn't promote women as often as men. It might be easier to fix an algorithm than…the minds of 10,000 store managers."
>
> RICHARD SOCHER

For context, Richard Socher is a top-cited natural language processing researcher. He is the founder and CEO of You.com, a search engine powered by a chatbot that competes with Open AI's ChatGPT, Google's Gemini, and Microsoft's Copilot.

AI bias can originate from various causes, with biased training data being a key factor. For example, facial recognition trained primarily on light-skinned faces will struggle with darker-skinned individuals. Bias can also arise during development, where developer choices, such as feature selection or problem framing, may introduce bias. Additionally, if fairness isn't considered in evaluation metrics, the model may perform well overall but poorly for specific groups.

Mitigating bias in AI requires deliberate and thoughtful strategies. One practical and effective approach is to use diverse and representative training datasets. Ensuring the data covers various scenarios and demographics can help the model learn more equitable patterns. For instance, an AI hiring tool should be trained on data that includes diverse candidates to avoid favoring any group. Bias detection and correction algorithms are also essential. These algorithms can identify and adjust for biases in the model's predictions. For example, fairness-aware machine learning techniques can reweight the data or change the decision thresholds to ensure fairer outcomes.

Several organizations are actively addressing AI bias. IBM has worked on reducing bias in its AI hiring tools by using diverse datasets and implementing fairness checks. Their open-source AI Fairness 360 toolkit, now managed by the Linux Foundation, includes bias mitigation algorithms and fairness metrics to help users detect and reduce bias in machine learning. Similarly, Microsoft's Fairlearn toolkit helps developers balance fairness with other performance metrics, aiding in more equitable decision-making. These efforts highlight the critical need for proactive approaches to build fair and unbiased AI systems.

AI AND JOB DISPLACEMENT: FINDING A BALANCE

AI's automation of repetitive and manual tasks is one of its most significant impacts on the job market and is changing the nature of work. Tasks such as data entry, customer service, and elements of manufacturing are the most common tasks AI systems perform, reducing the need for humans to undertake this work. AI-powered warehouse robots can, for example, sort and move products more efficiently than humans. Despite the obvious business benefits, such as increasing productivity and reducing operating costs, these advancements raise valid concerns about job displacement. Some traditional roles may very well become obsolete, creating a pressing need for workers to adapt.

While AI displaces some jobs, it also creates opportunities in AI-related fields. The technology industry is booming with roles such as data scientists, machine learning engineers, and AI ethicists. These positions require specialized skills and offer attractive career prospects.

To mitigate job displacement, reskilling and upskilling programs are crucial for providing workers with the tools they need to succeed in a labor market increasingly driven by AI. Governments and private organizations must invest in training initiatives focusing on digital literacy, coding, data analysis, and AI fundamentals. Online courses, coding boot camps, and professional certifications can help workers acquire these skills. Learning platforms like Coursera and edX offer AI and machine learning courses that are accessible to anyone with an internet connection. Providing access to quality education, these programs help workers transition to new roles, reducing the risk of unemployment.

Government policies also play a vital role in supporting workforce transition. Policymakers must create an environment that encourages continuous learning and skill development. This can include funding for education and training programs, incentives for businesses to invest in employee development, and support for displaced workers.

Education is a cornerstone in addressing job displacement. Integrating AI and technology courses into school curriculums prepares the next generation for future job markets. Early exposure to coding, data science, and AI concepts nurtures interest and proficiency in these fields. Schools must prioritize STEM (Science, Technology, Engineering, and Mathematics) education, ensuring students develop critical thinking and problem-solving skills. Lifelong learning initiatives are equally crucial for continuous skill development. Encouraging adults to pursue further education through workshops, online courses, and professional development programs ensures they remain competitive in an evolving job market.

Successful adaptation to AI is evident in various industries, such as manufacturing, which has embraced AI-powered machinery for assembly lines, quality control, and predictive maintenance. Many workers in these factories have transitioned to roles that involve overseeing AI systems, requiring technical skills and continuous learning.

RISKS AND RESPONSIBILITIES IN LAW ENFORCEMENT

Artificial intelligence is increasingly used in law enforcement. One of the primary applications is predictive policing algorithms. To help law enforcement prevent crimes before they happen, algorithms analyze historical crime reports, weather conditions, and social events to identify patterns and predict potential hotspots of criminal activity, helping law enforcement agencies appropriately redirect resources to these areas.

Facial recognition technology is another AI tool widely used in law enforcement. This technology can identify individuals by analyzing facial features captured in images or video footage. It is often employed in surveillance, border control, and identifying suspects in criminal investigations. Cameras equipped with facial recognition software can scan crowds at public events to identify individuals who are wanted by the police. While these applications can enhance security, they also raise significant ethical concerns.

Privacy violations and mass surveillance are top-of-mind ethical issues associated with AI in law enforcement. The pervasive use of facial recognition technology can lead to constant monitoring of individuals without their consent, infringing on their right to privacy. This kind of surveillance creates an environment of distrust and can be seen as an invasion of personal freedom. Furthermore, there is a risk of wrongful arrests and discrimination. If the AI systems are inaccurate or biased, they can misidentify individuals, leading to false accusations and legal consequences. This is particularly concerning for marginalized communities who may already face systemic biases.

To address these ethical concerns, it is crucial to establish frameworks for responsible AI use in law enforcement. Transparency and public accountability are vital components. Law enforcement agencies should be open about using AI technologies and the data they collect. This transparency builds public trust and ensures that AI systems are used responsibly. Regular audits and impact assessments are also essential. These evaluations help identify biases or inaccuracies in the AI systems and assess their impact on different communities. By conducting these assessments, agencies can make necessary adjustments to improve fairness and accuracy.

Real-life examples demonstrate the importance of responsible AI use in law enforcement. Some police departments have engaged communities in developing AI tools, seeking input and addressing concerns at the outset. This community engagement nurtures trust and ensures that AI applications align with public expectations. Additionally, adopting strict data privacy measures is vital. Some agencies have implemented protocols to ensure that data collected through AI systems is stored securely and used only for its intended purpose. These measures protect individuals' privacy and prevent misuse of their data.

FUTURE ETHICAL CHALLENGES

As AI technologies evolve, they bring forth new ethical dilemmas that demand our attention. One of the most pressing concerns is the use of AI in autonomous weapons and warfare. These systems can make life-and-death decisions without human intervention, raising questions about accountability and moral responsibility. The possibility of misuse by non-state actors or rogue states introduces another layer of complexity.

Ethical considerations in AI-driven decision-making systems extend beyond warfare to critical areas like healthcare and finance. For instance, an AI system making medical diagnoses or financial decisions must operate accurately and fairly. Any error or bias could severely affect people's health and economic well-being.

Proactive policymaking is essential to ensure that AI technologies are developed and used responsibly. Developing international AI ethics guidelines—like the principles of ethical AI used at the United Nations—can provide a standardized framework for ethical

AI practices. These guidelines should result from collaboration between governments, industry leaders, and academic institutions. Such collaboration ensures the guidelines are comprehensive, practical, and adaptable to different contexts. These stakeholders can address AI's multifaceted ethical issues by working together to support a global consensus on responsible AI use.

Establishing ethics committees and review boards can help monitor the ethical implications of AI technologies. These bodies can conduct regular assessments to identify emerging ethical issues and recommend necessary adjustments so ethical guidelines on the use of AI remain practical and relevant. This dynamic approach allows us to stay ahead of the curve and avoid potential ethical challenges, ensuring that AI technologies benefit society without causing harm.

Visionary perspectives on ethical AI offer valuable insights into the future landscape of AI ethics. Thought leaders and experts in the field emphasize the importance of maintaining a human-centric approach to AI development, and interviews with AI ethicists reveal a consensus on the need for transparency, accountability, and inclusivity in AI systems. Researchers predict that the ethical landscape of AI will become increasingly complex over the next decade and integrate further into our daily lives, suggesting ethical questions will extend to new domains and uses. These predictions underscore the importance of ongoing dialogue and collaboration to navigate the ethical challenges that lie ahead.

KEEPING AI ON TRACK

Before we conclude this chapter, I want to highlight a few key points raised in a recent address, 'Keeping AI on Track,' at the World Economic Forum's Annual Meeting of the Global Future Councils. Stanford Institute for Human-Centered Artificial Intelligence professor Erik Brynjolfsson raised several crucial points relevant to our current discussion on ethical AI. He explained that AI's future shouldn't focus on mimicking human intelligence. Instead, it should handle tasks humans aren't good at, like complex route optimization, leaving humans to excel in areas that machines can't, like personal interaction and caregiving, to name a couple of examples. In this way, both AI and humans bring unique strengths to the table.

He also raised awareness about the lack of investment in understanding AI's societal impact. Technology is progressing rapidly with advancements in software, hardware, and computational power. Yet, our social structures—laws, institutions, and economic systems—are not keeping pace, creating an ever-widening gap between the two. While it is promising to see advancements being made to close the gap (like the EU's introduction of the AI Act), much more must be done to keep AI in check.

Finally, Brynjolfsson also highlighted that AI's future is not predetermined. He underscored that our choices today will shape how AI evolves, so nothing about AI's trajectory is inevitable. In other words, while we are and will face ethical challenges with AI, we also have the power to control its use and how it advances.

* * *

CHAPTER 4 SELF-ASSESSMENT

Let's cap off this chapter with a quick quiz to help cement your understanding of what you have learned thus far. Scan the QR code below or visit this URL [**https://tinyurl.com/AICh4Quiz**].

QR code to access the Chapter 4 quiz.

MAKE A DIFFERENCE WITH YOUR REVIEW!

Help others unlock the power of machine learning, generative AI, and ChatGPT to advance their careers, boost creativity, and keep pace with modern innovations.

"No one has ever become poor by giving." — Anne Frank

People who give without expecting anything in return are often the happiest. So, let's spread some happiness together.

Would you help someone curious about AI figure out where to start? Let them know they can confidently engage with this topic by picking up a copy of *Essentials of AI for Beginners*. When you leave a review, you're helping others decide if this book is right for them. Your message could inspire:

…an entrepreneur to start their next big idea.
…an aspiring author to write their first book.
…a recent graduate to find a job they love.
…a retiree to discover a new hobby.

Leaving a review takes less than a minute but makes a big difference!

QR code to leave a review. URL:
https://geni.us/EssentialsofAI_PB

BONUS MATERIAL

Thank you very much for purchasing this book and leaving a review! Please scan the QR code below or type [**https://tinyurl.com/AIBonusMaterials**] into your internet browser to unlock exclusive bonus content, including descriptions and use cases for over 30 popular AI platforms and tools. These tools are categorized by their primary functions, including:

- Communication,
- Content creation and editing,
- Design and creativity,
- Development and data science,
- Marketing and sales,
- Personal finance and health,
- Productivity and automation,
- Visual analysis and search, and
- Virtual reality.

QR code to unlock exclusive bonus content.

FIVE
AI-ENHANCED CREATIVITY AND INNOVATION

Artificial Intelligence isn't only about crunching numbers and analyzing data; it's also a powerful tool for creativity and innovation. This chapter will explore how AI can boost your creative potential. Using examples and case studies, we'll dive into the exciting—and sometimes controversial—world of generating stunning art, composing beautiful music, and crafting compelling stories using AI.

GENERATIVE ART

Generative art is an exciting field where AI takes on the role of an artist, creating unique and original artworks. AI systems can produce art autonomously, using algorithms to generate patterns, colors, and forms from the abstract to the highly detailed. AI models like Generative Adversarial Networks (GANs) or neural style transfer are used to create art. Neural style transfer blends one image's style with another's content, creating a new, hybrid artwork. (Refer to Chapter 1 for a refresher on how GANs work.)

Artists and creators use various tools to generate art with AI. Dozens of apps and platforms help artists and aspiring artists boost their creativity, but some popular ones include DALL-E (built natively on ChatGPT), OpenArt.ai, and ImagineArt.

AI-generated art has already made its mark in the art world. A real-world example of AI-generated art making its mark is the "Portrait of Edmond de Belamy" by the French art collective Obvious. This painting was generated using a GAN trained on a dataset of more than 15,000 portraits painted between the 14th and 20th centuries. The styles and techniques of historic works of art influence the resulting image. AI generated the portrait, which Christie's auctioned in 2018 for a surprising US$432,500—far exceeding the estimated range of $7,000 to $10,000. This event sparked a discussion about ownership, the nature of creativity, and the role of AI in the art world.

A more recent example of AI-generated art making headlines is the rise of digital art created using tools like DALL-E, Midjourney, and Stable Diffusion. These tools allow artists to generate detailed, creative images based on text prompts. Jason Allen generated "Théâtre D'opéra Spatial" in 2022 and won first place in the "Digital Art/Digitally Manipulated Photography" category at the Colorado State Fair's annual art competition. The artwork was created using Midjourney, a leading AI tool that turns text descriptions into images. To make this piece, Allen provided Midjourney with text prompts describing a futuristic space opera scene. The AI tool generated multiple variations from which Allen selected and refined the final piece he submitted to the competition.

As I am sure you'd expect, the victory sparked debate in the art community. Critics argued that AI-generated art should not compete alongside human-created works, given the fundamentally different creative process involved. Supporters, however, pointed out that Allen's involvement in refining and selecting the final image meant it was a legitimate creative effort, not to mention the text prompts he generated for Midjourney to be able to execute his vision.

* * *

THE ART OF THE PROMPT

I'm certain you've seen many AI-generated images, whether you realize it or not. The quality of AI-generated images is so good it's often hard to discern what's real and what's been produced by AI. Images, text, and music generated by AI are based on prompts.

A prompt refers to the input or question given to an AI model to guide its output or response. In the context of ChatGPT, Claude, or Gemini, a prompt is the text, instruction, or query a user provides to initiate a response from the AI system. Many other AI-driven apps and platforms also use prompts to generate art, music, poetry, and more. Prompts come in different forms. For example, instructional prompts direct the AI on what to do, like "Explain what a tuple is in Python." Open-ended prompts encourage broader responses like "Tell me about the latest AI advancements." Clarifying prompts can be used to request clarification, like "Could you elaborate on that?"

Let's explore how prompts work by creating AI-generated art using the OpenArt platform. OpenArt creates images from text prompts, meaning you can instruct the AI to generate a specific image. Getting the AI to generate (output) an image that aligns with your vision takes practice. This practice of crafting and refining the textual prompts given to AI models is called prompt engineering. How you structure your prompts directly impacts the quality and precision of the image generated by the model.

A tale of two prompts

Consider "sunset over the ocean" versus "a vivid orange sunset over a calm ocean, with pink clouds scattered across the sky and gentle waves lapping at the sandy shore. The sun is halfway below the horizon, casting a warm glow across the water. In the foreground, sandpipers are scurrying about, searching for their next meal."

The first prompt is vague, so it's unlikely to generate an image that meets your vision. However, you will likely get much closer to your vision by using a more detailed prompt, like the second, which is a more improved and specific prompt. You can continue to revise your prompt until you get the image you want. The two AI-generated images shown below demonstrate the impact of prompt specificity.

AI-generated image from the vague prompt 'sunset over the ocean,' captures a general oceanic sunset scene. Created on the OpenArt platform, using the Kolors model.

AI-generated image from a more detailed prompt illustrates a more vibrant and intricate depiction featuring sandpipers on the shore at sunset. Created on the OpenArt platform, using the Kolors model.

AI-ENHANCED CREATIVITY AND INNOVATION 73

Activity: AI-generated Images

Try generating images yourself on the OpenArt platform! Visit the OpenArt website [**openart.ai**] and create an account. You'll receive free trial credits deducted each time you generate an image. If you enjoy the platform, you can buy more.

Select "+ Create Image" on the homepage, then choose an AI model like Stable Diffusion or Kolors. After selecting the model, enter your prompt. You can create your own or use the "vivid orange sunset" example.

Scan the QR code below or enter [**https://tinyurl.com/ AIHandsOnActivities**] into your browser for more prompts for you to experiment with, such as a SCUBA diving scene, a NASCAR race scene, wildflowers in a vase, jazz musicians in New Orleans, and more. You'll also find more information on ChatGPT basics to help you harness this powerful tool.

QR code to access the hands-on activities.

DALL-E is another excellent tool for generating images. It's built natively on ChatGPT, so if you have a paid ChatGPT account, you can type in a prompt for the image you want to create, and voilà! It's that simple!

A cubist-style image of a young black woman listening to music on her headphones on the subway. Generated using DALL-E.

WRITING WITH AI

AI is a powerful tool for writing, helping with idea generation, drafting, and editing. Large language models like GPT-4 are especially useful for generating coherent, contextually relevant content. AI-powered digital 'writing partners' are always ready to assist. ChatGPT can generate high-quality text based on text prompts, and you can refine the output by providing more precise instructions, such as asking it to use active voice and avoiding using specific terms or phrases. Its applications range from blog posts to full-length novels. Another popular tool, Anthropic's Claude, is praised for generating more "human-like" writing. ChatGPT and Claude offer free versions with premium options for enhanced features.

Several AI tools excel in the realm of creative writing. AI Dungeon, for example, offers an interactive storytelling experience where the AI helps you co-create stories in real-time. Sudowrite and Plot Generator are other tools designed to assist creative writers by providing suggestions, generating text to help overcome writer's block, and enabling you to explore new creative directions. ScriptBook is an AI tool with script analysis, content validations, and automated story generation. I recommend exploring these tools to see which grabs your attention. Most, if not all, of these tools allow you to explore them for free before making a financial commitment.

AI-assisted writing projects are becoming increasingly common. Some authors use AI to generate first drafts, which they refine and polish. This approach saves time and allows writers to focus on higher-level creative decisions. Collaborative novels written with AI assistance demonstrate the potential of this technology, blending human creativity with machine-generated content to produce unique literary works. AI-generated short stories and poems have also been well-received, offering fresh perspectives and imaginative ideas.

The difference between AI-generated and AI-assisted content lies in the degree of human involvement. AI-generated content involves minimal input from the author, while AI-assisted means using AI for brainstorming, editing, or refining text. Tools like Grammarly and Quillbot, which check spelling, grammar, sentence structure, tone, delivery, and even plagiarism, are examples of AI that are already widely used.

A recent real-world example of AI-generated literature is *1 the Road*, written by an AI developed by Ross Goodwin, a creative technologist and AI researcher. Goodwin embarked on a road trip across the U.S. with a car equipped with sensors, a GPS, a camera, and an AI model that generated text. The AI received visual data from the camera, geographical data from the GPS, and other inputs from the sensors as the car traveled from New York to New Orleans. Processing this data in real-time, the AI created text based on what it "saw" and "experienced" during the journey. Goodwin edited and compiled the text but did not alter the AI's output. The result includes a mix of poetry, prose, and stream-of-consciousness writing, reflecting the AI model's unique and often abstract perspective.

AI IN MUSIC COMPOSITION

AI tools like AIVA (Artificial Intelligence Virtual Artist) are revolutionizing music by generating music in various styles, including classical, jazz, and pop, and even composing complex orchestral pieces.

AIVA and tools like it enable you to choose a style like old-school rap, folk rock, or techno or use an influence like a chord progression or an existing audio file. AIVA generates a track based on your selections, which you can customize by adjusting the tempo, melody, chords, and instrumentation. It's an ideal tool for people who want extensive control over their compositions, and its interface is beginner-friendly.

AI-generated music is now widely used in film scores and advertising. In film, AI helps composers by generating initial soundtrack drafts, which are later refined to match the movie's tone. In advertising, AI creates tailored jingles to engage specific audiences.

A recent collaboration between AI and musicians is the project "A.I. Song Contest," an international music competition designed to showcase the creative potential of human-AI co-creativity. This annual event began in 2020 and is hosted in different places, such as Hilversum, Netherlands, where the inaugural event occurred. The Synthetic Beat Brigade, composed of music producers, AI specialists, and musicians, won the 2023 AI Song Contest for their song "How would you touch me?" Another notable song is "Beautiful the World" by the team Uncanny Valley from Australia. This remarkable song is unique as it was generated by a neural network trained on audio samples from well-known Australian animals such as koalas, kookaburras, and Tasmanian devils. These, plus the other winning songs, are worth a listen. You can do so on the AI Song Contest website [**www.aisongcontest.com**].

QR code to access the AI Song Contest website.

AI IN GAME DEVELOPMENT

AI enhances game design by creating intelligent and responsive non-player characters (NPCs). AI-powered NPCs can adapt to your actions, offering dynamic and immersive gameplay. For example, Machine Learning Agents is an open-source toolkit offered by Unity Technologies. It enables developers to create intelligent agents within the Unity game engine, allowing them to learn and adapt to different scenarios. Behavior trees and state machines help define NPC behaviors, ensuring they act believably and engagingly. Reinforcement learning will enable NPCs to improve their performance through trial and error, creating more challenging and rewarding gameplay experiences.

Companies like Ubisoft, known for games like *Assassin's Creed*, *Far Cry*, and *Rainbow Six* continue to advance gaming technology. During the 2024 Game Developer's Conference in San Francisco, Ubisoft showcased its NEO NPC AI technology, which introduced cutting-edge features like memory, situational awareness, decision-making, and emotional responses. These advancements push gaming toward more natural, immersive experiences, blurring the line between reality and fantasy.

Released in 2020 after many delays, *Cyberpunk 2077* by CD Projekt Red immediately faced controversy, including glitches that obscured characters' faces and exposed their private parts. The developer released several updates, fixing the glitches and improving

NPC behavior. Now, NPCs react more realistically to player actions, such as fleeing danger, forming crowds, and responding based on the player's notoriety. NPCs can also recognize if the player is wielding a weapon and respond by attacking, fleeing, or calling for help. These improvements and more complex daily routines for NPCs have set a new standard for immersion in open-world games. Developers now look to *Cyberpunk 2077's* updated NPC behavior as a benchmark for creating more interactive gaming environments.

MEET AI-DA

Let me introduce you to Ai-Da in this chapter. Ai-Da is an ultra-realistic humanoid robot who also happens to be an artist. She can draw and paint using AI algorithms, her robotic arms, and the cameras in her eyes. Her artistic capabilities don't end there, as Ai-Da is also a performance artist, poet, and designer. Ai-Da was "born" (created) in 2019 and has captivated audiences with her talent ever since. "Unsecured Futures" was Ai-Da's first solo exhibit, from June 12 to July 8, 2019, at St. John's College at the University of Oxford. There, Ai-Da showcased her drawings and performance art. Other notable appearances have been at the United Nations AI for Good global initiative in May 2024, and her thought-provoking discussions have even reached the UK Parliament's House of Lords. See for yourself what Ai-Da's all about by visiting her website [**www.ai-darobot.com**].

QR code to access Ai-Da's website where you can view her exhibitions.

INNOVATING WITH AI

AI is driving innovation across industries, including automotive. BMW's concept car, iX Flow, uses AI and E-Ink technology to allow drivers to change the car's exterior color with the touch of a button. E-Ink, also known as electrophoretic display technology, works by suspending millions of microcapsules containing black, white, and color pigments in a thin film, each of which is differently charged. When an electric field is applied, specific pigments rise to the surface, changing the car's color. This process allows the vehicle to shift shades, offering a dynamic and customizable exterior.

AI algorithms control these color changes, adjusting based on factors like the driver's mood or the weather. Beyond offering personalization, the technology has practical uses, such as switching to high-visibility colors in poor weather for safety or adopting subtler tones in urban environments to reduce attention. This blend of AI and E Ink represents a leap forward in vehicle personalization and functionality.

In the beauty industry, Yves Saint Laurent's Rouge Sur Mesure Custom Lip Color Creator lets users create custom lipstick shades using PERSO technology developed by L'Oréal Group. Unveiled at the 2021 Consumer Technology Association tradeshow, PERSO uses AI to analyze factors like skin type, environmental conditions, and user preferences to create personalized beauty products on demand. The Rouge Sur Mesure device connects to an app via Bluetooth. Beyond custom lip colors, PERSO technology can offer personalized skincare and foundations. This innovation helps brands like YSL build stronger customer relationships and opens opportunities for subscription services, offering tailored refills or new formulations based on ongoing skin analysis.

Even in agriculture, AI is making an impact. John Deere has integrated AI and machine learning into its products to modernize farming. The company's focus on precision agriculture and autonomous machinery has led to innovations like AI-powered autonomous tractors that can plow, plant, and harvest without a driver. John Deere also uses AI for precision farming, analyzing data from satellite imagery, sensors, and soil samples to provide actionable insights. Another key innovation is their See & Spray technology. It uses AI and computer vision to identify weeds and apply herbicides only where needed, reducing chemical use and costs while minimizing environmental impact.

* * *

CHAPTER 5 SELF-ASSESSMENT

Are you curious about how well you've absorbed the information in this chapter? Take the quiz that will put your knowledge to the test. Access it by scanning the QR code below, or entering [**https://tinyurl.com/AICh5Quiz**] into your browser.

QR code for the Chapter 5 quiz.

SIX
CAREER PATHWAYS IN AI

Artificial Intelligence is no longer just for computer scientists. Educators, marketers, healthcare workers, bankers, farmers, entrepreneurs, artists, and so many more professions are seeing just how vital AI skills are for their careers. Such skills are increasingly becoming necessary, whether you want to change careers or grow in your current role.

THE IMPORTANCE OF AI LITERACY

AI is transforming the world of work. More and more companies recognize the benefits of using AI, and those whose workforces embrace and are up-to-speed with AI tools and technologies have much to gain. For this reason, developing AI literacy for nearly all working people will become increasingly imperative, much like knowing how to use the Microsoft Office suite of products (Word, Excel, PowerPoint, etc.) is now a "given" for those working in office environments. However, AI literacy should considered as a spectrum. Not everyone needs to be an expert in Python coding, and all of us don't need a data science or machine learning background to excel. But, we do need to have an appropriate level of knowledge and competence to continue to thrive in our careers. For example, a marketing professional might not need Python coding experience, but other roles—like medical researchers—might. Examining your current role and evaluating where AI fits into it and what competencies you might need to develop to keep pace with technological advancements is essential. So, as you continue reading this chapter, don't assume you need to transition into an AI career, but do assume that developing an appropriate level of AI literacy for your role is necessary.

TRANSITIONING INTO A CAREER IN AI

The roadmap to entering the AI field is clear and accessible, even if you start with no technical background. The first step is establishing a strong foundation in AI vocabulary and concepts like those we explored in earlier chapters. Other excellent starting points are reading more books and taking online courses offered by Coursera or edX. Such educational platforms provide structured learning paths that guide you from beginner to more advanced levels, often with hands-on projects reinforcing your understanding.

Next, focus on acquiring practical skills, like learning more about Python, one of AI development's most widely used programming languages. Begin with the Python basics, then learn specialized libraries like TensorFlow for machine learning and NLTK for natural language processing. You've already dipped your toes in the water, so to speak, if you undertook the practice activities in Chapter 3, but of course, there's much more to explore. Practical experience is vital, so consider participating in hackathons or coding competitions to apply your skills in real-world scenarios. These events enhance your coding abilities and provide networking opportunities for other AI enthusiasts and professionals.

The approach is slightly different if you want to incorporate AI into your current profession. Begin by identifying tasks in your work that could benefit from AI. If you're a marketer, this might mean using AI to analyze customer data to predict buying patterns and optimize advertising strategies. If you're a healthcare worker, you might use AI applications to improve diagnoses or to streamline administrative work to free up your time to attend to patients. If you're a banker, you might use AI to provide more customized investment solutions to your clients or analyze data from various sources to better appreciate market sentiments. The goal is to pinpoint repetitive or data-intensive tasks that AI can streamline or enhance. Once identified, seek AI tools and platforms tailored to your job or industry. Many sectors now offer AI solutions that don't require extensive programming knowledge, making integrating AI into your workflow much more straightforward.

Consider enrolling in industry-specific AI courses focusing on practical applications relevant to your field. These courses often provide case studies and examples demonstrating how AI can solve relatable challenges. Additionally, keep yourself up-to-date with the latest AI trends and developments by attending webinars and conferences and engaging with professional networks that can offer insightful information and assist you in staying abreast of modern innovations and AI advancements.

Lastly, embrace the idea of continuous learning. This is so important that this book devotes an entire chapter to it. We'll explore this topic further in Chapter 7.

EXPLORING AI JOBS

In the dynamic field of AI, understanding different job roles can help you identify where your skills and interests align. A Data Scientist, for instance, focuses on data analysis and modeling. They clean, analyze, and interpret complex datasets to provide actionable insights. They often use statistics, programming, and data visualization tools to make sense of large volumes of data. A typical day in the life of a Data Scientist involves performing exploratory data analysis and building predictive models. At a tech company, for example, a Data Scientist might analyze user behavior data to improve product features, enhancing user experience and retention rates.

A Machine Learning Engineer, on the other hand, concentrates on developing and implementing machine learning models. They serve as an essential bridge between data science and software engineering by focusing on creating scalable and efficient models. Their work includes training models, tuning hyperparameters (settings defining machine learning models' structure and operation), and deploying models into production. They need a strong software engineering background and be proficient with machine learning frameworks such as TensorFlow and PyTorch. For example, a Machine Learning Engineer working on a recommendation system for an e-commerce platform might develop algorithms to suggest products based on user preferences and past behavior, significantly boosting sales and customer satisfaction.

Through their innovative and cutting-edge research, AI Research Scientists focus on pushing the limits of what's possible with AI. Their work involves conducting literature reviews, developing new algorithms, and publishing their findings in academic journals. This role requires advanced knowledge of mathematics, research methodologies, and deep learning techniques. An AI Research Scientist at a university, for instance, might work on a project to develop new neural network architectures that improve image recognition accuracy, contributing to the scientific community and advancing the field of AI.

An AI Ethicist plays a key role in ensuring that AI systems are designed and used responsibly. They focus on identifying and addressing ethical concerns like bias, privacy, and transparency. They collaborate with developers, policymakers, and legal teams to implement ethical frameworks and guidelines. For example, an AI Ethicist at a social media company might evaluate how AI-driven content recommendation systems influence public discourse, ensuring these algorithms don't promote misinformation or polarizing content while balancing ethical concerns like free expression and public engagement.

The people who oversee the development and deployment of

AI-driven products and solutions are AI Product Managers. Their job is to ensure that AI solutions meet business goals and user needs. Their responsibilities include defining product requirements, coordinating between engineering and design teams, and managing the product lifecycle. They need strong project management skills, good communication skills, a solid understanding of AI concepts, and business acumen. For example, an AI Product Manager at a startup company might oversee the development of a new AI-powered app, ensuring it meets market demands and user expectations while staying within budget and timeline constraints.

Case Study: Maurice McKenny - Revolutionizing Fintech with AI

Maurice McKenny, a Stanford-trained data scientist, left a major financial institution to join Technova Solutions, a fintech startup aiming to serve underbanked populations. His challenge? Develop an AI-powered mobile app offering personalized financial advice, savings plans, and credit-building strategies.

Maurice tackled multiple hurdles head-on. He built a scalable cloud-based data pipeline to integrate information from various sources. Using Python, Scikit-Learn, and TensorFlow, he developed predictive models for credit score improvement and savings goal recommendations. A personalization tool helped users stay more engaged by recommending financial products they might like based on similar users' choices.

Regulatory compliance wasn't overlooked. Maurice implemented robust encryption and security measures to meet GDPR and CCPA standards. He also adopted an iterative development approach, refining the app through A/B testing and user feedback.

The results were impressive. Within six months, the app gained over 100,000 active users who reported significant improvements in their financial health. Underbanked users, in particular, benefited from actionable steps toward financial stability. The app's success sparked investor interest and garnered innovation awards for the company.

Maurice's work at Technova demonstrates the power of AI and data science in democratizing financial services. By creating meaningful, scalable solutions, he's helping to bridge the gap for underserved communities and reshape the fintech landscape.

ESSENTIAL SKILLS FOR AI CAREERS

To thrive in an AI career, you need technical and non-technical skills. The technical skills you will need will vary depending on your position, but it's safe to assume proficiency in programming languages like Python and R is a must. While Python is the most widely used language, R is also valuable, particularly for statistical analysis and data visualization. You'll also need to be knowledgeable about database modeling and data warehousing and be able to use data processing tools like Pandas and NumPy, which help you manipulate and analyze large datasets. Knowledge of Intelligent User Interfaces (IUI) and machine learning fundamentals are core requirements for many AI-related jobs.

If this all sounds intimidating to you, I get it. However, rest assured that acquiring these skills is doable. Rather than looking at all the skills required and thinking they're impossible to achieve, start your learning journey by taking one step at a time. Since AI jobs are among the most in-demand, this has led to a surge in brick-and-mortar educational institutions offering tailored programs for people looking to transition into an AI-related career. And, of course, there's a plethora of online courses, degrees, and certificates in these and other technical competencies required for a job in AI. These educational programs are designed to meet your needs and fit your schedule, whether working or studying full-time or taking a break from work.

Various non-technical skills are also required to succeed in an AI role. Problem-solving and critical thinking skills are vital because AI often involves tackling complex challenges without straightforward solutions. Thinking creatively is necessary to develop effective algorithms and models. Teamwork is also essential, as AI projects typically involve cross-functional teams, including data scientists, engineers, and business analysts. Having excellent communication skills is vital; this cannot be overstated. Communicating your ideas clearly in collaborative work environments is crucial, and communication skills are also essential when discussing your work with business executives, potential users of the programs you're developing, clients, and more. Project management and time management skills help you keep projects on track, ensuring deadlines are met and resources are used efficiently.

Transitioning into an AI career requires a blend of personal traits that support learning, adaptability, and perseverance. These fundamental traits include intellectual curiosity, resilience, patience, open-mindedness, and embracing lifelong learning.

NETWORKING IN THE AI COMMUNITY

Networking in the AI community is pivotal in career growth and development. Cultivating business relationships can open doors to opportunities that might not otherwise present themselves and often provide insights into industry trends, upcoming projects, and emerging technologies. Networking also facilitates collaboration on research and practical projects, allowing you to work with experts in the field and gain valuable experience. Engaging with peers and mentors can result in collaborative project opportunities that help you build your professional portfolio and improve your skills, making you a more attractive candidate to employers.

Many AI conferences offer excellent opportunities for learning, networking, and staying updated on AI innovations. Examples include:

- *NeurIPS* (Conference on Neural Information Processing Systems), held annually in December, focuses on machine learning, AI, and computational neuroscience. It's one of the largest AI conferences, typically hosted in the US or Canada.
- *ICML* (International Conference on Machine Learning), hosted every June or July in cities worldwide, features

groundbreaking research on AI, machine learning, and deep learning.
- *AI World Conference & Expo*, held annually in Boston in October, emphasizes AI in business and industry applications.

AI meetups present another excellent networking opportunity. These informal gatherings, where people interested in AI convene to exchange knowledge, build connections, and collaborate on projects, can range from small group discussions to more significant events with guest speakers, workshops, or presentations on AI-related topics. You can find such meetups on platforms and websites such as Meetup.com, Eventbrite, social media, and university or tech community boards.

Hackathons are competitive events where individuals or teams work on developing a project—often related to AI, coding, or tech—within a short time frame, usually 24-48 hours. They provide a high-energy environment where participants can showcase their skills, learn new technologies, collaborate with others, and sometimes win prizes. Hackathons are great for building portfolios, gaining hands-on experience, and connecting with potential employers or collaborators. You can find hackathons on websites and platforms, including Devpost, a widely used platform to find and participate in hackathons, both online and in person; Hackathons.io, a directory of upcoming hackathons worldwide; and social media and tech forums. Follow tech influencers on LinkedIn, X, or Reddit to stay informed about upcoming hackathons. Also, many colleges and universities host hackathons, which are often open to the public.

PREPARING FOR AI JOB INTERVIEWS

There are many things you can do to prepare for AI job interviews well before you're invited to one. Networking in the AI community and building a strong online presence (such as on LinkedIn) are the best ways to position yourself for a future interview. Research various companies you're potentially interested in working for and review multiple job descriptions for AI-related jobs to get a solid sense of what employers seek. Practice your responses to common AI interview questions, and brush up on AI, machine learning, and deep learning concepts.

Depending on the role you're applying for (such as data scientist, software engineer, or machine learning engineer) and the position level (such as entry-level or supervisor), the interview questions you'll face will differ. Some AI-related interview questions you could be asked include:

- What is artificial intelligence, and what are its applications?
- Tell me about a real-world AI application you find interesting.
- How do you stay updated on the latest trends and advancements in artificial intelligence?
- What are some of the challenges and ethical implications of AI?
- What role does machine learning play in AI?
- How would you explain the difference between AI, machine learning, and deep learning to someone without a technical background?

More technical questions might include:

- Explain the difference between model accuracy and model performance.
- What is the purpose of data normalization? Explain how a GAN works.
- What is the difference between supervised and unsupervised learning?
- Describe the process of hyperparameter tuning and its importance in optimizing machine learning models.

Advanced AI roles will require you to demonstrate your coding skills and understanding of specific functions, libraries, and more.

For instance, you could be asked to write a Python function to sort a list of numbers using the merge sort algorithm or implement a function to calculate precision, recall, and F1-score given an input of actual and predicted labels.

Many of the terms and concepts included in these questions have been discussed throughout this book. Also, if you engaged with the hands-on activities in Chapter 3, you will have developed a greater understanding of how these concepts are implemented. You may not be ready for an AI interview tomorrow, but you will succeed with continued learning, practice, and patience.

This may go without saying, but don't hesitate to use AI-powered tools to help prepare a job application or for an interview. For example, there are a plethora of resume-building tools you can use. If the job you're applying for requires a cover letter, you can ask an AI, like ChatGPT, to help with that, too. Also, try to include as many keywords from the job description in your application as possible, given AI's increasing role in hiring processes. For instance, Applicant Tracking Systems (ATS) are used to screen resumes and rank them well before human intervention.

Typically, interviews for AI roles are divided into several stages. The initial phone screen is your first hurdle. A recruiter or hiring manager will assess your qualifications and fit for the role. Expect questions about your background, experience, and interest in the organization. This stage is relatively straightforward but crucial for making a solid first impression.

Following the phone screen, you'll likely face technical assessments and coding challenges; again, this depends on the role you're applying for and its level. These tests evaluate your problem-solving abilities and technical skills. You might be asked to solve coding problems on platforms like LeetCode or HackerRank. These problems often focus on algorithms and data structures, requiring you to write efficient, clean code. Additionally, you may encounter case studies or real-world scenarios where you'll need to apply machine learning techniques. Reviewing common algorithms, practicing coding problems, and participating in mock interviews can significantly boost your performance. Whiteboard exercises are another typical component of technical interviews. During a whiteboard exercise, candidates are asked to solve a problem or demonstrate their thought process by writing code, algorithms, or diagrams on a whiteboard or a digital equivalent, like a virtual whiteboard in online interviews. Although such exercises can be intimidating, they are excellent for demonstrating your thought process and problem-solving skills clearly and logically.

Behavioral interviews are the next step, assessing your non-technical skills and cultural fit within the organization. The STAR method—Situation, Task, Action, Result—is a popular model used to structure responses. For example, you might be asked to provide an account of a complex project you worked on. In this example, discuss the situation or problem you faced, outline the tasks you were responsible for, explain your actions, and highlight the results. Emphasize teamwork, conflict resolution, and leadership experiences, as these qualities are highly valued in collaborative environments.

I'll leave you with one final thought before we continue further. Coaching may not be for everyone, but it can be extremely helpful. The lessons and techniques learned in such coaching sessions are transferrable; they can be used in any interview scenario. Finding an interview or career coach with a technical background could be beneficial; however, I have also had fantastic results with career coaches who don't necessarily specialize in the industry, and several of my friends and colleagues have, too. Coaching can be a lengthy and expensive process, depending on your needs. Still, if you're interviewing for a job that pays significantly higher than your current one (as many technical roles do) and has the potential to lead to more opportunities in the future, it could very well be worth the investment.

* * *

CHAPTER 6 SELF-ASSESSMENT

It's time to challenge yourself with the end-of-chapter quiz—a great way to reinforce learning. Scanning the QR code below will take you there, or enter [**https://tinyurl.com/AICh6Quiz**] into your browser.

QR code for the Chapter 6 quiz.

SEVEN
A JOURNEY OF LIFELONG LEARNING

As has been well established throughout this book, AI is a constantly evolving field that offers endless opportunities for growth, creativity, and innovation. Embracing lifelong learning in AI is not just a choice but a necessity, as it allows you to stay relevant, adapt to new methodologies, and remain competitive in an ever-changing landscape.

WHY LIFELONG LEARNING MATTERS

Breakthroughs in machine learning, computer vision, and natural language processing occur frequently in the AI field; thus, it is critical to continuously update your skills. Lifelong learning in AI is about more than just keeping up with new tools—it's about embracing change and innovation. By committing to this mindset, you position yourself as a forward-thinking professional, ready to adapt to new challenges and deliver innovative solutions as AI integrates into various industries.

Setting learning goals and creating a study plan helps support an outlook that values continuous learning. Start by identifying specific areas of AI that interest you or are relevant to your career or job you'd like to have, then break down these areas into manageable learning objectives and set realistic timelines. For instance, if you aim to master the Python programming language, you might set goals to complete specific online courses, read certain books, or work on Python projects within a set timeframe. This structured approach keeps you focused and motivated. The number of times I've encountered students and working professionals who want to master coding within a matter of weeks is unrealistic and can lead to demoralization. Being patient, consistent, and persistent in learning such skills is essential. And the importance of regular practice cannot be overstated.

Another effective strategy is leveraging online courses, workshops, and certifications for lifelong learning. Platforms like Coursera, edX, and Udacity offer many AI courses tailored to different skill levels and interests. Industry experts design these courses and provide hands-on experience through projects and assignments. Certifications from one or more of these platforms can help improve your CV and show your commitment to continuous learning.

As discussed in Chapter 6, engaging with AI communities and professional networks is equally important. Being part of a community allows you to share knowledge, seek advice, and collaborate on projects. Online forums, local AI meetups, and study groups offer opportunities to network and learn from peers in a more personal setting. These interactions can provide insights and motivation, making learning more enjoyable and effective.

People have different learning styles, so finding resources that suit your preferences is essential. Video tutorials on platforms like YouTube or specialized AI learning sites can be incredibly helpful if you are a visual learner, as they often provide step-by-step guides and visual aids that make complex concepts easier to understand. For auditory learners, podcasts are an excellent resource. Some excellent podcasts I'd recommend exploring include:

- *TWIML AI Podcast* (This Week in Machine Learning and AI) features interviews with AI researchers, practitioners,

and industry experts, covering the latest advancements in machine learning, deep learning, and AI.
- *AI Alignment Podcast* focuses on AI safety, ethics, and alignment, with discussions on the societal impact of AI and how to ensure its beneficial use.
- *Data Skeptic*, which explores machine learning, AI, and data science topics in an accessible way, often discussing practical applications and current trends.
- *Talking Machines* provides insights into machine learning research, expert interviews, and conversations about current issues in the field.

If you prefer hands-on learning, there are many popular interactive coding platforms where you can learn programming through practical exercises and projects, such as Codecademy and FreeCodeCamp. The former is a subscription-based platform that offers interactive courses in various programming languages and topics. It's well-suited for beginners and intermediate learners who like a clear, structured learning path. The latter is a free, community-driven platform offering a more project-based approach with hands-on learning in web development, Python, data science, and machine learning. The Khan Academy is another entirely online educational platform. It is well known for providing free, world-class education to learners of all ages. It offers a variety of subjects, including math, computer science, and more, through instructional videos, practice exercises, and personal learning dashboards.

At this stage, it's important to introduce you to Kaggle. Along with Google Colab, Kaggle is one of the essential platforms in the data science and machine learning community. Kaggle is known for hosting data science competitions, providing access to many datasets (including the iris dataset we used for one of our hands-on projects in Chapter 3), and promoting a community for learning and sharing insights. It's particularly famous for competitions where participants tackle real-world problems using data science techniques. Kaggle also offers a cloud-based environment for creating and sharing Jupyter Notebooks.

AI research journals and publications like *arXiv* and the *Journal of Artificial Intelligence Research* (JAIR) are invaluable for those interested in cutting-edge research. Cornell University maintains *arXiv*, which is widely respected in the academic and research community for its role in accelerating the dissemination of scientific knowledge. JAIR is another of the leading journals in the AI field. It's known for its rigorous peer review process and high-quality publications, which researchers and AI practitioners frequently refer to for the latest advancements.

Finally, professional organizations and conferences (such as NeurIPS and ICML) also play a crucial role in lifelong learning. Joining organizations like the Institute of Electrical and Electronics Engineers (IEEE) and the Association for Computing Machinery (ACM) provides access to exclusive resources, including research papers, webinars, and networking events.

TIME MANAGEMENT FOR BUSY LEARNERS

Many, if not most, would say we're too busy to learn about AI. The "I'm too busy mentality" is a major roadblock to learning and is one of the main excuses people use to avoid engaging in a complex topic. This is why busy people like us must create a realistic learning schedule, which is the cornerstone of effective time management, especially when balancing AI studies with other responsibilities. Start by allocating specific time slots for studying AI. These slots should be consistent and fit seamlessly into your daily routine. For example, dedicating an hour before work might be ideal for a morning person. Conversely, night owls might find late evenings more productive. The key is to find a time when you can focus without interruptions. This consistency helps form a habit, making sticking to your study plan easier.

Balancing AI learning with other responsibilities requires setting achievable goals. Break down your learning objectives into manageable tasks. Instead of aiming to complete an entire course in a week, set smaller, more realistic targets like finishing one module or chapter each week. This approach makes the task less daunting and provides a sense of accomplishment as you achieve these milestones. Celebrating these small victories can motivate you and give you a sense of progression, reinforcing your commitment to lifelong learning.

Maximizing learning efficiency is crucial when time is limited. The Pomodoro Technique, for example, involves breaking your work or study sessions into focused intervals, typically 25 minutes long, separated by short breaks. It works like this: choose a task you want to work on. This could be studying a specific concept, writing code, or reading. Set a timer for 25 minutes (this interval is called a Pomodoro, hence the technique's name). Work for the 25-minute interval, focusing only on the task you've chosen to work on. It's essential to avoid all distractions during this time. When the timer goes off, take a short break. Step away from your workspace when taking a break. Then, start another Pomodoro session, break, and repeat. After completing four Pomodoros, take a longer break, like 15-30 minutes. This will give you a sufficient break to recharge.

The fixed 25-minute intervals, or Pomodoros, create a sense of urgency to help you focus on the task and be productive. The regular breaks in between intervals help prevent burnout and mental fatigue. This technique is also helpful in tracking and managing time spent on tasks, making managing your workload and other priorities easier.

Here's how you might put this technique into practice:

- *First Pomodoro:* Read through a theoretical example and concepts to understand the foundation of an algorithm.
- *Second Pomodoro:* Apply the theory by practicing the implementation of the algorithm in code.
- *Third Pomodoro:* Review any errors or challenges you encountered and identify areas for improvement.
- *Fourth Pomodoro:* Summarize what you've learned and take notes to reinforce what you've practiced.

Incorporating AI learning into your daily routine can make the process more seamless and less overwhelming. Take advantage of idle times, such as commutes or lunch breaks, to engage with AI content. Listening to AI podcasts on your commute can provide insights and keep you updated on the newest advancements and trends. Similarly, reading AI articles during lunch breaks can help you stay informed without dedicating extra time outside your regular schedule. These minor adjustments can significantly increase your learning time without feeling like an additional burden.

TIPS AND TRICKS TO STAY MOTIVATED

Understanding your motivation for learning AI is essential for staying engaged. Start by linking your AI learning to specific career goals. For example, mastering core AI concepts can lead to new job opportunities and higher salaries if you aim to become a data scientist. For marketers, AI can improve how you analyze consumer data, resulting in better campaign strategies. Connecting your AI skills to professional growth makes learning more purposeful and rewarding.

Use your passions to power your AI journey. If you're fascinated by art, dive into generative models and watch your creativity soar. If you love writing, experiment with AI tools to elevate your craft. By aligning AI with your interests, you'll transform learning from a chore into something you look forward to. This personal connection fuels your motivation, keeping you engaged even when concepts get challenging.

It's natural to hit periods of low motivation. One effective strategy to overcome these is to vary your study routine. If you've been focusing heavily on theoretical aspects, switch to hands-on projects or vice versa. This change can reignite your interest and make the learning process more dynamic. Reading about individuals who have achieved significant milestones in AI despite facing obstacles can remind you that your efforts are worthwhile and can provide a motivational boost.

Having a support system in place is vital for maintaining motivation. Finding study partners or mentors can help keep you accountable and encourage you to stay on track. Study partners can share resources, provide different perspectives, and make learning more interactive. Mentors can offer guidance, answer your questions, and share their experiences, helping you navigate challenges more effectively.

Rewarding yourself for your progress is another effective way to stay motivated. Setting up a reward system for achieving learning milestones can provide the extra push you need to complete challenging tasks. No matter how small the reward is, it reinforces positive behavior, helping you build momentum to keep pushing forward with your learning.

As we wrap up this chapter, remember that lifelong learning in AI is a continuous process that requires dedication, effective time management, and sustained motivation. Your commitment to learning will enhance your skills and keep you at the forefront of this rapidly evolving field.

* * *

CHAPTER 7 SELF-ASSESSMENT

Take a moment to tackle the end-of-chapter quiz, accessible via the QR code below or this URL [**https://tinyurl.com/AICh7Quiz**].

QR code for the Chapter 7 quiz.

EIGHT
AI MISUNDERSTOOD

Despite AI's growing influence in our daily lives, many misconceptions about AI persist. These misunderstandings can lead to unrealistic expectations or unfounded fears of this technology. Setting the record straight is crucial, especially as AI becomes more omnipresent.

COMMON MISCONCEPTIONS ABOUT AI

1. AI is sentient.

Many people mistakenly believe that AI systems have consciousness and emotions akin to the human mind due to their advanced capabilities that mimic human behavior. This is a common misconception, especially with the rise of AI-driven robots like Ai-Da, which can perform impressive tasks like painting or holding conversations. However, even the most advanced AI lacks true self-awareness, emotions, or the ability to think independently; instead, AI systems follow algorithms and process vast amounts of data to complete tasks—they do not "feel" or "think" in any way comparable to humans. This distinction is essential, as conflating AI with human-like consciousness can lead to unrealistic expectations of what AI can do, not to mention ethical concerns.

2. AI can do everything a human can.

While AI excels in specific tasks like data analysis and pattern recognition, it lacks the general intelligence that humans possess. An AI system might be able to beat a grandmaster at chess but won't understand the social nuances of a casual conversation. AI systems are designed for narrow tasks and can't replicate the full spectrum of human abilities.

3. AI will replace all human jobs.

There's growing concern that AI will lead to massive unemployment by automating tasks traditionally performed by humans. While it's true that AI and automation are transforming industries, they are unlikely to replace all human jobs. Instead, AI is more likely to complement human work by automating repetitive or data-intensive tasks, allowing people to focus on higher-level, creative, or emotionally driven work. For instance, AI can streamline administrative tasks in a healthcare setting, but doctors and nurses will still be needed for patient care and decision-making. New jobs in AI ethics, oversight, and integration are also emerging as AI becomes more embedded in our lives. While the job landscape will shift, human creativity, emotional intelligence, and complex problem-solving skills will remain invaluable.

4. AI is infallible.

AI is often perceived as flawless because of its reliance on data and algorithms, but in reality, AI systems are far from perfect. They can make mistakes, especially if trained on biased, outdated, or incomplete data. For example, an AI model used in hiring may inadvertently favor certain demographics if the training data reflects existing societal biases. These biases can manifest in various ways, from lending decisions to criminal justice. Continuous oversight and improvement of AI models are necessary to minimize errors. AI tools like ChatGPT can provide valuable assistance, but users should always verify the information before fully relying on it. Blindly trusting AI-generated content without checking for accuracy can lead to unintended consequences, so research and critical thinking are still essential.

5. AI learns independently like a human.

While AI can improve its performance through learning algorithms, it doesn't learn in the intuitive, experiential manner that humans do. AI relies on large datasets and predefined rules to make decisions. It can't draw from personal experiences or understand context like humans. This limits its ability to adapt to entirely new situations without additional data and reprogramming.

6. AI has independent thought.

Unlike humans, AI doesn't have beliefs, desires, or intentions. It follows programmed instructions and lacks the capability for independent thinking. For instance, a navigation app can provide the fastest route based on traffic data, but it doesn't care whether you reach your destination. It's vital to recognize that AI operates within the confines of its programming.

7. AI can understand all contexts and nuances.

Despite significant advancements in natural language processing (NLP), AI still struggles with understanding context and nuance. AI-powered chatbots and virtual assistants may perform well with straightforward tasks, but they often falter when faced with complex or ambiguous language. For example, an AI might misinterpret sarcasm, irony, or cultural references because it doesn't grasp the underlying tone or intent. Context is a uniquely human trait that relies on shared experiences, emotions, and situational awareness, which AI hasn't fully mastered yet.

8. AI is always objective.

AI systems can inherit biases present in their training data. Facial recognition software, for example, might perform worse on darker-skinned individuals if it's primarily trained on lighter-skinned faces. Objectivity in AI depends heavily on the quality and diversity of the data it learns from.

9. AI will lead to a robot apocalypse.

This fear is often fueled by science fiction movies where AI systems turn against humanity. In reality, AI development is increasingly regulated and monitored to prevent such scenarios. The focus is on creating AI that benefits society, not harms it. Also, robots are not synonymous with AI. AI refers to the intelligence in machines that can perform tasks, whereas robots are physical entities that may or may not use AI to operate.

10. AI can make moral decisions.

AI algorithms can follow ethical guidelines set by programmers, but they lack the inherent understanding of morality that humans possess. For example, an autonomous car might be programmed to minimize harm in an accident, but it doesn't "understand" the moral implications of its decisions.

11. AI will continuously improve over time.

While AI systems can become more accurate with more data and better algorithms, they aren't guaranteed to improve indefinitely. For instance, data quality, computational power, and algorithmic design limitations can hinder progress. Continuous innovation and ethical oversight are essential to ensure AI evolves beneficially.

12. All AI products are 'smart.'

Companies often exaggerate AI capabilities, contributing to common misconceptions. The Federal Trade Commission warns businesses against overstating what AI products can do. Products like smart thermostats or fridges are often labeled 'intelligent' or 'smart,' but they don't operate autonomously and should, therefore, be called 'connected.' Some companies also claim their products use AI when AI was only part of the development process. Claims that AI products are better than non-AI alternatives should be backed by evidence, as this isn't always the case. Such overstated claims can lead to the false belief that AI is superior in all contexts.

13. AI is only for tech giants and tech-savvy people.

This couldn't be further from the truth, and I hope this book helped, at least in part, to dispel this misconception. AI development is now more accessible than ever, thanks to open-source tools, platforms, and resources that allow anyone with a computer and a stable internet connection to get started. Small businesses, researchers, and everyday people can leverage AI to create projects, develop apps, and enhance their skills—often without extensive technical expertise. AI is no longer confined to large corporations or experts; it's becoming a tool everyone can explore and utilize.

14. AI and automation are the same.

While AI and automation are often confused, they are distinct concepts. Automation involves programming systems to perform repetitive tasks based on predefined rules. These systems don't adapt or learn from experience; they follow instructions. On the other hand, AI involves systems that can learn from data, adapt to new information, and make decisions. AI can power automation, but it goes beyond basic tasks by handling more complex, unpredictable scenarios. Essentially, automation is about doing tasks more efficiently, while AI is about making systems intelligent enough to improve and evolve.

15. AI systems are inherently secure and immune to hacking.

Many believe that AI systems, due to their complexity, are secure by default, but this is far from true. Like any software, AI systems can be vulnerable to cyberattacks, data breaches, and manipulation. If an AI system is not properly secured, it can be exploited by malicious actors who can manipulate the algorithms or data inputs to cause incorrect outcomes. Additionally, AI systems often rely on large datasets, making them targets for data theft or adverse data manipulation, where corrupted data skews the system's performance. Security measures must be actively implemented and maintained for AI systems to remain secure.

* * *

CHAPTER 8 SELF-ASSESSMENT

See how much of this chapter you've absorbed by taking the short end-of-chapter quiz. Access it by scanning the QR code below or this URL [**https://tinyurl.com/AICh8Quiz**].

| QR code for the Chapter 8 quiz.

NINE
PREPARING FOR THE FUTURE

As AI continues to evolve, it's crucial to understand emerging trends and technologies that will shape the future. From integrating AI with quantum computing to advancing autonomous systems and natural language understanding, the next wave of AI innovations promises to revolutionize how we approach complex problems, manage urban living, and tackle environmental challenges. This chapter discusses these emerging trends, emphasizing the need for adaptability, continuous learning, and proactive preparation to thrive in an AI-driven world.

EMERGING TRENDS: WHAT'S NEXT?

Quantum Computing and Quantum AI

The integration of AI with quantum computing is an exciting development. Quantum computing uses the unique behaviors of tiny particles, like atoms, to handle information differently from regular computers. Normal computers store and process data as 0s and 1s, but quantum computers use " qubits." Qubits, short for quantum bits, are quantum computers' fundamental units of quantum information. Qubits can represent a 1 and 0 simultaneously, processing data much faster. Therefore, when combined with AI, quantum computing can process data faster and solve highly complex problems much quicker.

Building stable quantum computers remains a challenge. However, once that's overcome, fields like cryptography, financial modeling, and drug discovery could be revolutionized in ways we can only theorize by performing calculations at unprecedented speeds. For now, much of Quantum AI (QAI) and Quantum Machine Learning (QML) is still theoretical, but this rapidly emerging field is garnering significant investment from the likes of Google, IBM, and Microsoft, so it's unlikely it will remain conceptual for much longer.

Quantum computing and its integration with AI are hot topics, leading companies like Google to launch competitions like XPRIZE Quantum Applications to speed up development. XPRIZE is a three-year global competition with a five-million-dollar prize purse. The competition has been designed to encourage the next generation of quantum computing algorithms to help solve real-world global challenges in climate, sustainability, health, and more.

AI-Powered Autonomous Systems

Another groundbreaking trend is the advancement of AI-powered autonomous systems. Such systems or machines can perform tasks or make decisions independently using AI. They're designed to perceive their environment, process information, and take actions based on that information to achieve specific goals. Characteristics of AI-powered autonomous systems include:

- *Sensing and perceiving.* These systems use sensors, including cameras, LiDAR, short for Light Detection and Ranging, and radar to sense and perceive.
- *Understanding the environment, predicting outcomes, and making decisions* that could involve navigation, object detection, or undertaking complex tasks.

- *Utilizing actuation and control* by controlling hardware components like motors or robotic arms.
- *Learning and adapting.* These systems learn and adapt continuously to improve their performance over time as they encounter new data and experiences.

The application of AI-powered autonomous systems goes well beyond self-driving vehicles, though these systems are already making significant waves in transportation. Some top autonomous vehicle companies include Mobileye, NVIDIA, Qualcomm, Valeo, and Waymo. Each of these companies is a pioneer as they work to develop systems that can navigate complex urban environments safely and reliably and deliver on the promise of reducing traffic accidents, lowering emissions, and enhancing mobility for those unable to drive. Despite the regulatory and other hurdles this technology faces, these promised benefits make this an area ripe with opportunities for innovation.

Unmanned aerial vehicles, used in military, agriculture, and delivery services, are other examples on the rise. Autonomous robots, used in manufacturing, healthcare, and other industries for tasks like assembly, surgery, and logistics, are further applications of this technology.

Advancements in Natural Language Understanding

Advances in Natural Language Understanding (NLU) are also shaping the future of AI. NLU is a branch of AI focusing on a machine's ability to comprehend and interpret human language. It is a crucial NLP (Natural Language Processing) component, enabling computers to understand human communication's nuances, context, and intent. NLU underpins many conversational AI systems, such as customer service chatbots and virtual assistants. Enhanced NLU can improve customer service by providing more accurate and context-aware responses, reducing the need for human intervention. However, perfecting NLU requires overcoming difficulties like understanding idiomatic expressions and cultural nuances, which are inherently complex and varied.

Many exciting advancements are being made in NLU. For example, transformer models such as BERT (Bidirectional Encoder Representations from Transformers) allow models to understand the context of a word based on all surrounding words in a sentence. This bidirectional approach improves sentiment analysis, question answering, and text classification. GPT (Generative Pre-trained Transformer), primarily known for text generation, also has strong NLU capabilities. It can understand context, maintain coherent dialogue, and perform tasks like summarization and translation. Pre-trained Language Models, such as RoBERTa, T5 (Text-To-Text Transfer Transformer), and ALBERT, are variants of transformer models fine-tuned for specific NLU tasks, improving the efficiency and accuracy of language understanding across various applications.

Zero-shot and few-shot learning are techniques used in AI models that allow them to perform tasks they haven't explicitly been trained on. These models can understand instructions given in everyday language, making them flexible for many functions.

Other exciting advancements include multimodal NLU. Multimodal NLU allows AI to combine text with other data types, like images or sound, to better understand what's being asked.

Finally, contextual and conversational understanding improvements enable AI systems to handle longer conversations more effectively, remember previous interactions, and manage more complex discussions.

AI FOR A SMARTER, SAFER, AND MORE SUSTAINABLE FUTURE

The Role of AI in Our Cities

Smart (or connected) cities represent a forward-thinking approach to urban living. These metropolitan areas use interconnected systems and data-driven insights to manage resources efficiently, improve public services, and encourage a more livable environment. At the heart of smart cities lies AI, which plays a crucial role in collecting, analyzing, and acting on data to solve complex urban challenges. As cities continue to grow, the need for AI-driven solutions becomes even more crucial to ensure smooth operations and sustainability.

AI's involvement in smart city infrastructure is multifaceted. In traffic management, AI-driven systems analyze real-time data from cameras, sensors, and GPS devices to optimize traffic flow and reduce congestion. By adjusting traffic signals dynamically and providing alternative routes, AI helps mitigate traffic jams, reduce commute times, and lower emissions. Similarly, AI-powered energy management systems monitor and control energy usage across the city. These systems predict demand patterns, optimize energy distribution, and integrate renewable energy sources, significantly reducing energy consumption and its associated carbon footprint.

Waste management is another area where AI makes a significant impact. Connected waste management systems use AI to monitor bin waste levels and optimize collection routes. This ensures bins are emptied efficiently, reducing fuel consumption and operational costs. AI can also analyze waste composition to inform recycling efforts and reduction strategies.

The benefits of AI in smart cities extend beyond efficiency and sustainability. AI enhances public transportation by predicting demand and optimizing routes, ensuring that buses and trains run on time and serve the most needed areas. Public safety also sees improvements through AI-driven surveillance systems that detect unusual activities and alert authorities in real-time, enabling faster response to emergencies.

Of course, the widespread adoption of AI in our cities raises important ethical and privacy concerns, such as data privacy and security, which we examined in Chapter 4. Additionally, equitable access to connected, AI-powered technologies must be guaranteed to prevent the digital divide from widening. Balancing innovation with community input and transparency is essential to building trust and ensuring that AI-driven solutions benefit all residents equally.

AI in Environmental Applications

AI technologies enhance environmental monitoring and disaster response. AI-powered early warning systems detect signs of natural disasters like earthquakes, floods, and hurricanes, providing timely alerts to minimize damage and save lives. Remote sensing and AI also offer real-time monitoring of environmental changes through satellite imagery, tracking deforestation, glacier melting, and ocean acidification. Additionally, AI systems monitor air and water quality, identifying pollutants and sources of contamination, enabling prompt corrective actions.

AI supports decision-making for environmental policies. Governments and organizations can use AI to assess the effectiveness of policies aimed at reducing greenhouse gas emissions. AI models evaluate the outcomes of different policy choices, such as shifting from fossil fuels to renewable energy or implementing a carbon tax. These insights help policymakers make informed decisions.

Resource optimization is another area where AI makes a significant impact. In supply chains, AI analyzes data to streamline logistics, reduce emissions, and minimize waste. Intelligent building management systems use AI to optimize energy consumption by monitoring heating, cooling, and lighting. AI also improves industrial processes by identifying inefficiencies and recommending ways to reduce resource use and emissions.

Promoting a circular economy, where resources are reused and recycled rather than discarded, is another area where AI excels. AI-driven design tools create products with recyclability in mind, extending their lifecycle and reducing waste. Powered by AI, predictive maintenance ensures that machinery is serviced before failures occur, prolonging its usability. In waste sorting and recycling facilities, AI improves accuracy and efficiency. AI also supports the sharing economy by optimizing resource usage, as seen in platforms like Uber, Bolt, and Lyft, which use AI to match drivers with riders efficiently.

Biodiversity conservation benefits from AI as well. AI-powered wildlife monitoring systems track animal movements, aiding anti-poaching efforts and protecting species. AI analyzes images from camera traps to identify species and estimate populations, providing data for conservation strategies. Additionally, AI monitors environmental conditions and predicts the success of habitat restoration efforts.

As with any technology, AI's use in environmental applications brings challenges. Ensuring accuracy in AI-driven models is critical, as inaccurate predictions can lead to misguided policies. Addressing biases in AI systems is essential to avoid ecological injustice, where vulnerable communities bear the brunt of environmental impacts. Balancing data collection with privacy concerns and minimizing ecosystem disruption are also challenges.

Energy consumption is another growing concern. AI models require large amounts of energy to operate, with data centers being a major contributor to global energy consumption. To illustrate just how energy-intensive Large Language Models like ChatGPT are, each time you ask ChatGPT something, that query uses ten times more energy to process than a Google search! Also, the International Energy Agency estimates that 2022 data center electricity use accounted for about 1 to 1.3% of global electricity demand. The good news is tech companies like Google, Meta, and Microsoft are working toward carbon neutrality in digital infrastructure, including data centers, through initiatives like the iMasons Climate Accord. Furthermore, the rising use of AI is helping to ignite the rapid development of alternative energy sources, such as wind, solar, nuclear, and geothermal.

Human-AI collaboration is vital in environmental efforts. AI serves as a tool to support decision-making, offering data-driven insights for policy and conservation strategies. Citizen science initiatives, where volunteers contribute to data collection, can be enhanced with AI for more accurate environmental monitoring. Blending AI solutions with traditional ecological knowledge ensures that technology complements indigenous and local expertise, fostering sustainable environmental protection.

Cybersecurity and AI

As cyber threats evolve, the need for AI-driven solutions becomes increasingly critical. AI helps in proactive measures, such as threat detection and prevention, and reactive measures, like incident response and mitigation. By leveraging AI more efficiently and effectively, cybersecurity professionals can identify and counteract threats faster and more precisely.

In threat detection and prevention, for example, AI excels at identifying anomalies in network traffic. Machine learning models can detect and classify malware by analyzing patterns that indicate malicious behavior. Predictive analytics further enhance security by identifying potential vulnerabilities before they can be exploited. Real-time threat intelligence gathering and analysis allow for immediate responses to emerging threats, ensuring that security measures are always up-to-date.

AI also plays a crucial role in automated incident response, significantly enhancing the speed and efficiency of addressing cyber-attacks. AI-driven systems can triage and prioritize security alerts, ensuring that the most critical threats are addressed first. Automated containment and remediation tools can isolate compromised systems and neutralize threats without human intervention. Additionally, AI assistants help security analysts streamline investigations, providing valuable insights and reducing the time needed to respond to incidents.

User and entity behavior analytics (UEBA) is another area where AI shines. By establishing baseline behavior patterns, AI can continuously monitor user activities and detect subtle changes that may indicate insider threats or compromised accounts. This continuous analysis helps identify and mitigate risks that traditional security measures might miss. For example, an AI system can flag unusual login times or access to sensitive data as potential red flags.

Offensive cybersecurity is all about preventing an attack before it happens. AI enhances penetration testing and red team exercises, a cybersecurity assessment method where security professionals (the Red Team) simulate a real-world attack on an organization's systems, networks, or physical security to identify vulnerabilities and weaknesses before hackers or other cybercriminals exploit these weaknesses first.

There are examples of several notorious hackers who now help networks and computer systems become more secure. A few notable cases include the late Kevin Mitnick, one of the most infamous hackers in the 1980s and early '90s who, after serving time in prison for his high-profile hacking activities, founded Mitnick Security Consulting, where he provided penetration testing services and security consulting to organizations worldwide. A more recent example is Marcus Hutchins, known for stopping one of the most significant cyberattacks in history, the 2017 WannaCry ransomware attack. WannaCry infected and destroyed the data of hundreds of thousands of computers worldwide. Hutchins stopped this attack by finding and triggering the "kill switch" hidden deep within its code. Before this heroic act that some say "saved the internet," Marcus created and sold malware, most famously the Kronos banking trojan, for which he was arrested by the FBI in 2017. Today, he's a globally known and respected cybersecurity expert and speaker.

Despite its benefits, AI in cybersecurity also poses challenges, as I am sure you can imagine. For example, malicious actors can leverage AI to enhance their capabilities, such as generating sophisticated phishing attacks or using adversarial machine learning to evade detection systems. Automated tools can also discover and exploit vulnerabilities at a scale and speed previously unimaginable, amplifying the potential impact of cyber-attacks. These advancements necessitate continuous innovation in defensive technologies to keep pace with evolving threats.

Human-AI collaboration is vital in cybersecurity. AI acts as a force multiplier, augmenting the capabilities of human security analysts and allowing them to focus on strategic decision-making. Human oversight and judgment remain crucial to ensure security measures are applied appropriately and ethically. Training and adapting the cybersecurity workforce for an AI-driven landscape is vital to exploit AI's benefits while mitigating potential risks.

BUILDING RESILIENCE IN AN AI-DRIVEN WORLD

Personal resilience becomes crucial for navigating the changes brought on by AI. Adapting to rapid technological evolution means being open to learning new skills and staying updated with the latest developments. AI's impact on job markets and industries is significant, with many roles evolving or becoming obsolete. Resilience in this context involves being proactive about upskilling and reskilling to remain relevant in the workforce. Maintaining mental and emotional well-being is also vital. Rapid changes can be stressful, and building resilience helps you manage this stress and adapt positively.

Building resilience involves several actionable steps. Earlier, we talked about creating an attitude of continuous learning and skill development. We looked at ways to engage with AI, such as online courses and workshops, local AI meetups, and more. It is also vital to embrace flexibility and adaptability. Be open to new opportunities and willing to pivot when necessary. Viewing challenges as opportunities for growth rather than obstacles can significantly impact your ability to adapt and thrive.

To thrive in an AI-driven world, you need to develop certain skills, even if you're not planning to become a data scientist, machine learning engineer, or computer programmer. All of us should have at least a basic understanding of AI and machine learning concepts. This knowledge will help you grasp how AI systems work and their potential applications, which is needed as AI's influence and impact continue to grow. Digital literacy is also vital. Being proficient with AI tools and platforms can give you a significant advantage, whether using AI-powered software at work or connected devices at home. Critical thinking and problem-solving skills are equally important as they enable you to assess AI applications critically, understand their limitations, and make informed decisions about their use.

Incorporating AI into your daily routine can be straightforward and rewarding. Use AI assistants for time management and organization. Set reminders, schedule meetings, and even ask for daily briefings to stay on top of your tasks. Utilize AI-powered health and fitness apps to keep track of your physical activities, monitor your health metrics, and receive personalized wellness advice. Implement AI budgeting and financial planning tools to gain insights into your spending habits and optimize your savings. These practical steps can enhance your productivity and well-being, making AI an integral part of your everyday life.

Adapting to AI comes with its fair share of challenges, but these can be overcome with the right approach. One common obstacle is the fear and misconceptions surrounding AI, many of which were discussed in Chapter 8. Educating yourself and others about what AI can and cannot do, dispelling myths, and understanding its capabilities are essential. Also, always use your best judgment. While AI can handle many tasks efficiently, human judgment and ethical considerations should always guide its use. By staying informed and vigilant, you can navigate the complexities of AI and make the most of its advantages.

* * *

CHAPTER 9 SELF-ASSESSMENT

To reinforce what you've learned in this chapter, scan the QR code below or enter [**https://tinyurl.com/AICh9Quiz**] into your browser to take a short quiz!

QR code for the Chapter 9 quiz.

CONCLUSION

If reading this book was one of your first forays into AI, I'm grateful to have been your guide.

Our AI journey has been eye-opening. We started by building a solid foundation, unpacking the terminology and core concepts that power AI. We explored how AI, machine learning, and deep learning fit together, forming the backbone of this technology.

Next, we witnessed AI in action, transforming industries from healthcare to finance and retail to entertainment. We saw its potential to reshape education, empower entrepreneurs, and simplify our daily lives.

But we didn't just observe; we created. Through hands-on coding and prompt-based activities, we built projects—from a simple calculator and trivia game to lifelike AI-generated images.

We also tackled the critical questions surrounding AI ethics: How do we ensure fairness, transparency, and privacy? How do we mitigate bias? These issues remind us that responsible AI development is grounded in our values as much as it is in technology.

The world is overflowing with AI opportunities. From data scientists and machine learning engineers to AI ethicists, there are countless ways to build a rewarding career in this field. Maintaining curiosity and committing to lifelong learning is essential. From online courses to local meetups, we explored numerous ways to continue evolving and staying at the forefront of AI innovation.

We dispelled common AI myths and glimpsed into the future of this technology—exploring emerging trends like quantum computing, autonomous systems, advancements in natural language processing, and AI's growing roles in urban planning, environmental protection, and cybersecurity.

As we come to a close, thank you for joining me on this journey. My passion for making complex topics accessible and my positive experiences with AI drove me to write this book. I hope it has inspired you and given you the confidence to embrace AI and continue experimenting and learning.

Let me leave you with a few final thoughts. First, AI isn't just for advancing careers—it's a powerful tool for enhancing creativity and personal projects and driving innovation. While ethical challenges exist, AI is helping solve some of our most pressing global issues. Use it ethically, wisely, and creatively as you continue your exploration. Second, in this digital, AI-driven age, always remember you are important. Humans create, train, and oversee AI systems. We set the policies, give feedback, and decide when and how AI should be used. We control how deeply it integrates into our lives. Finally, you've taken the first steps toward AI literacy and its practical use—an achievement worth celebrating. Embrace AI with confidence, creativity, and, most of all, curiosity.

> *The important thing is not to stop questioning. Curiosity has its own reason for existing. One cannot help but be in awe when one contemplates the mysteries...of life, of the marvelous structure of reality. It is enough if one tries to contemplate only a little of this mystery every day.*
>
> ALBERT EINSTEIN

THANK YOU

Thank you again for reading *Essentials of AI for Beginners*. I hope you enjoyed it as much as I enjoyed writing it.

If you haven't already done so, I'd appreciate it if you could leave a review of this book. Doing so will help others discover this book, which could make a meaningful difference in their lives.

Leaving a review takes less than a minute!

Please scan the QR code below and leave your review, or enter this link into your browser: [**https://geni.us/EssentialsofAI_PB**]

With gratitude,
Melissa

| QR code to leave a review.

GLOSSARY

This book introduced you to many AI terms, concepts, tools, and other resources. To aid in your continued learning, I've included a comprehensive glossary of terms. Please scan the QR code below to access it, or enter [**https://tinyurl.com/AIGlossaryofTerms**] into your browser.

QR code to access the comprehensive glossary.

REFERENCES

Admin-Science. (2024, January 24). Understanding the domain of artificial intelligence. *AI Blog*. https://mmcalumni.ca/blog/understanding-the-boundaries-and-possibilities-of-the-artificial-intelligence-domain

AI Fairness. (2020, October 2). Home - AI Fairness 360. AI Fairness 360. https://ai-fairness-360.org/

AI Pro. (2024, July 2). The top AI resources for learning: Courses and online platforms. *AI-Pro*. https://ai-pro.org/learn-ai/articles/the-top-ai-resources-for-learning-courses-and-online-platforms/

AI Song Contest. (n.d.). AI Song Contest 2024. https://www.aisongcontest.com/

Aigerim, M. (2023). Sales forecasting and demand planning with analytics. *Modern Scientific Technology*, (4). Retrieved from https://ojs.publisher.agency/index.php/MSC/article/view/2099

Akif, S. (2023, October 7). Case study: How Netflix uses AI to personalize content recommendations and improve digital marketing. *Medium*. https://medium.com/@shizk/case-study-how-netflix-uses-ai-to-personalize-content-recommendations-and-improve-digital-b253d08352fd

Alvi, F. (2024, January 24). PyTorch vs TensorFlow in 2024: A comparative guide of AI frameworks. *OpenCV*. https://opencv.org/blog/pytorch-vs-tensorflow/

Andre, D. (2024, August 20). RunwayML review 2024: Is it the best AI video tool? *All About AI*. https://www.allaboutai.com/ai-reviews/runwayml/#best

Arcas, B. A. Y. (2023, October 10). Artificial general intelligence is already here. *NOEMA*. https://www.noemamag.com/artificial-general-intelligence-is-already-here/

Archana, M. K., Prasad, D. V., & Ashok, M. (2024). Blockchain and AI-enabled new business models and applications. https://doi.org/10.58532/v3bgba1p6ch1

Atleson, M. (2023, February 27). Keep your AI claims in check. *Federal Trade Commission*. https://www.ftc.gov/business-guidance/blog/2023/02/keep-your-ai-claims-check

Australia - Uncanny Valley. (n.d.). VPRO International. https://www.vprobroadcast.com/titles/ai-songcontest/teams/australia.html

Aixploria. (n.d.-a). AI tools directory. Aixploria. https://www.aixploria.com/en/

Aixploria. (n.d.-b). Best AI tools for human resources. Aixploria. https://www.aixploria.com/en/category/human-resources-ai/

Baskin, K. (2023, September 15). The age of AI: Seven things entrepreneurs need to know. *Babson Thought & Action*. https://entrepreneurship.babson.edu/age-of-ai-for-entrepreneurs/

Bremmer, I. (2024, January 8). The top 10 global risks for 2024. *TIME*. https://time.com/6552898/top-10-global-risks-for-2024/

BriteWire. (n.d.). Neural networks. https://britewire.com/neural-networks/

REFERENCES

Brynjolfsson, E. (2024, October 16). *Betazone: Keeping AI on track* [Speech]. Annual Meeting of the Global Future Councils. World Economic Forum. https://www.weforum.org/events/annual-meeting-of-the-global-future-councils-2024/sessions/keeping-ai-on-track/

Box, B. (2023, December 15). Cybernetic travel nursing: Enhancing patient care and addressing the medical professional shortage. *Night Box*. https://nightbox.ca/cynet-travel-nursing/

Brown, S. (2024, January 17). How generative AI is changing entrepreneurship. *MIT Sloan*. https://mitsloan.mit.edu/ideas-made-to-matter/how-generative-ai-changing-entrepreneurship

Cardillo, A. (2024, October 1). 20 most popular AI tools ranked (September 2024). *Exploding Topics*. https://explodingtopics.com/blog/most-popular-ai-tools

Cardona, M., Rodríguez, R. J., Ishmael, K., & U.S. Department of Education. (2023). Artificial intelligence and the future of teaching and learning. https://www2.ed.gov/documents/ai-report/ai-report.pdf

Chandra, A. L. (2022, September 27). McCulloch-Pitts Neuron: Mankind's first mathematical model of a biological neuron. *Medium*. https://towardsdatascience.com/mcculloch-pitts-model-5fdf65ac5dd1

Chen, Y., & Huang, S. Y. (2016, May 10). The effect of task-technology fit on purchase intention: The moderating role of perceived risks. *Journal of Risk Research*, 20(11), 1418–1438. https://doi.org/10.1080/13669877.2016.1165281

Cohen, A. (2024, May 24). AI is pushing the world toward an energy crisis. *Forbes*. https://www.forbes.com/sites/arielcohen/2024/05/23/ai-is-pushing-the-world-towards-an-energy-crisis/

Conte, N. (2024, January 24). Ranked: The most popular AI tools. *Visual Capitalist*. Retrieved June 15, 2024, from https://www.visualcapitalist.com/ranked-the-most-popular-ai-tools/

Costa, A. (n.d.). Scientific writing with generative artificial intelligence: Innovation vs integrity. *Ludomedia*. Retrieved August 20, 2024, from https://en.ludomedia.org/qnow-scientific-writing-with-generative-ai/

Council of the European Union. (2024, May 21). Artificial Intelligence (AI) Act: Council gives final green light to the first worldwide rules on AI. https://www.consilium.europa.eu/en/press/press-releases/2024/05/21/artificial-intelligence-ai-act-council-gives-final-green-light-to-the-first-worldwide-rules-on-ai/

Coursera. (n.d.). Andrew NG, Instructor. https://www.coursera.org/instructor/andrewng

Cowell, A. (2019, June 5). Overlooked no more: Alan Turing, condemned code breaker and computer visionary. *The New York Times*. https://www.nytimes.com/2019/06/05/obituaries/alan-turing-overlooked.html

Cuizon, A., Jr. (2023, August 9). The impact of artificial intelligence on entrepreneurship. *Medium*. https://medium.com/@alcuizonup/the-impact-of-artificial-intelligence-on-entrepreneurship-4429446bb6c9

Davenport, T., & Kalakota, R. (2019). The potential for artificial intelligence in healthcare. *Future Healthcare Journal*, 6(2), 94–98. https://doi.org/10.7861/futurehosp.6-2-94

Dedicated Art Ltd. (n.d.). Ai-Da. *Ai-Da*. https://www.ai-darobot.com/

REFERENCES

Dennis, M. A. (2024, August 5). Marvin Minsky: AI pioneer, cognitive scientist & MIT professor. *Encyclopedia Britannica*. https://www.britannica.com/biography/Marvin-Lee-Minsky

DigitalDefynd. (2024, July 13). 10 AI in healthcare case studies [2024]. *DigitalDefynd*. https://digitaldefynd.com/IQ/ai-in-healthcare-case-studies/

Duhatschek, P. (2024, October 5). How power-hungry AI could help fuel growth in alternative energy. *CBC*. https://www.cbc.ca/news/canada/calgary/artificial-intelligence-power-alternative-energy-1.7343074

Edmond, C. (2019, August 5). 10 of Albert Einstein's best quotes. *World Economic Forum*. https://www.weforum.org/agenda/2019/08/albert-einstein-quotes-inspiring-clever-funny-famous/

Elgersma, C. (2024, March 6). ChatGPT and beyond: How to handle AI in schools. *Common Sense Education*. https://www.commonsense.org/education/articles/chatgpt-and-beyond-how-to-handle-ai-in-schools

Ernst & Young. (2024, March 6). Overcoming AI anxiety. *WIRED*. https://www.wired.com/sponsored/story/overcoming-ai-anxiety/

European Parliament. (2023, August 6). EU AI Act: First regulation on artificial intelligence. *European Parliament*. https://www.europarl.europa.eu/topics/en/article/20230601STO93804/eu-ai-act-first-regulation-on-artificial-intelligence

Fairlearn. (n.d.). About us. https://fairlearn.org/v0.10/about/index.html

Fatima, F. (2024, June 27). Top 7 AI music generator tools of 2024. *Data Science Dojo*. https://datasciencedojo.com/blog/ai-music-generator/

Feng, T., Jin, C., Liu, J., Zhu, K., Cheng, Z., Lin, G., & You, J. (2024, May 16). How far are we from AGI? *arXiv*. https://arxiv.org/abs/2405.10313

Fitzgerald, A. (2024, May 6). AI in cybersecurity: How it's used + 8 latest developments. *Secureframe*. https://secureframe.com/blog/ai-in-cybersecurity

Frank, A. (2020, December 18). How one of the biggest games of 2020 became one of the most controversial. *Vox*. https://www.vox.com/culture/22187377/cyberpunk-2077-criticism-ps4-xbox-one-bugs-glitches-refunds

Geneva Science and Diplomacy Anticipator. (n.d.). Human augmentation - GESDA science breakthrough radar. *GESDA*. https://radar.gesda.global/trends/human-augmentation

Germain, T. (2024, June 18). AI took their jobs. Now they get paid to make it sound human. https://www.bbc.com/future/article/20240612-the-people-making-ai-sound-more-human

Goldman Sachs. (2024, May 14). AI is poised to drive 160% increase in data center power demand. *Goldman Sachs*. https://www.goldmansachs.com/insights/articles/AI-poised-to-drive-160-increase-in-power-demand

Greenberg, A. (2020, May 12). The confessions of Marcus Hutchins, the hacker who saved the internet. *WIRED*. https://www.wired.com/story/confessions-marcus-hutchins-hacker-who-saved-the-internet/

Griffiths, S. (2016, August 26). Signs of cancer can be identified by AI software 30 times faster than doctors. *WIRED*. https://www.wired.com/story/cancer-risk-ai-mammograms/

Gupta, S. (2024, January 29). The top 5 AI programming languages you need as an AI engineer. *Springboard*. https://www.springboard.com/blog/data-science/best-programming-language-for-ai/

Hamilton, I. (2024, June 6). Artificial intelligence in education: Teachers' opinions on AI in the classroom. *Forbes Advisor.* https://www.forbes.com/advisor/education/it-and-tech/artificial-intelligence-in-school/

Hamirani, Q. (2024, February 20). Here's how generative AI will redefine the workplace. *Forbes.* https://www.forbes.com/sites/qhamirani/2024/02/15/heres-how-generative-ai-will-redefine-the-workplace/

Heads of State and Government & United Nations. (2024). Pact for the future. In *United Nations Summit of the Future: Our Common Agenda.* https://www.un.org/sites/un2.un.org/files/sotf-the-pact-for-the-future.pdf

High-Level Committee on Programmes, Inter-Agency Working Group on Artificial Intelligence (IAWG-AI), & Chief Executives Board for Coordination. (2024). United Nations system white paper on AI governance: An analysis of the UN system's institutional models, functions, and existing international normative frameworks applicable to AI governance. *UN System Chief Executives Board for Coordination (CEB).* https://unsceb.org/united-nations-system-white-paper-ai-governance

Hinduja, P. (2024, July 24). 10 best plot generators for powerful storytelling in 2024. *PaperTrue.* https://www.papertrue.com/blog/plot-generators/

Hodgson, J. (2023, March 9). Top 5 autonomous vehicle companies we recently studied. *ABI Research.* https://www.abiresearch.com/blogs/2023/03/09/top-autonomous-vehicle-companies/

Hosny, A., Parmar, C., Quackenbush, J. et al. (2018). Artificial intelligence in radiology. *Nat Rev Cancer* 18, 500–510. https://doi.org/10.1038/s41568-018-0016-5

IBM. (n.d.). AI vs. machine learning vs. deep learning vs. neural networks. *IBM.* https://www.ibm.com/think/topics/ai-vs-machine-learning-vs-deep-learning-vs-neural-networks

IBM. (n.d.). What is strong AI? *IBM.* https://www.ibm.com/topics/strong-ai

iMasons Climate Accord. (2024, August 9). iMasons Climate Accord – Carbon neutrality in digital infrastructure. *iMasons.* https://climateaccord.org/

International Energy Agency. (n.d.) Data centres & networks - IEA. *International Energy Agency.* https://www.iea.org/energy-system/buildings/data-centres-and-data-transmission-networks

International Energy Agency, Gas, Coal and Power Division. (2024). Electricity 2024. *International Energy Agency.* https://iea.blob.core.windows.net/assets/6b2fd954-2017-408e-bf08-952fdd62118a/Electricity2024-Analysisandforecastto2026.pdf

InfoSoft. (n.d.). A journey through the history of artificial intelligence. https://infosoft.ua/history-of-ai

International Telecommunication Union. (n.d.). Artificial intelligence for good. *International Telecommunication Union (ITU).* https://aiforgood.itu.int/

Jenengevik. (2024, August 19). OpenArt vs. Imagine.art: Which AI tool is better? *Perplexity.* https://www.perplexity.ai/page/openart-vs-imagine-art-compari-krfsJ4ieQn.SOob3Jv2cHA

REFERENCES

John Deere. (n.d.-a). Precision ag technology. Retrieved August 26, 2024, from https://www.deere.com/en/technology-products/precision-ag-technology/

John Deere. (n.d.-b). See & spray ultimate: Targeted in-crop spraying. https://www.deere.com/en/sprayers/see-spray-ultimate/

John Deere. (n.d.-c). The next giant leap in ag technology. Retrieved August 26, 2024, from https://www.deere.com/en/autonomous/

Jones, J. (2018, October 26). A portrait created by AI just sold for $432,000. But is it really art? *The Guardian.* https://www.theguardian.com/artanddesign/shortcuts/2018/oct/26/call-that-art-can-a-computer-be-a-painter

Kaggle. (n.d.). Find open datasets and machine learning projects. *Kaggle.* https://www.kaggle.com/datasets

Karjian, R. (2023, August 16). The history of artificial intelligence: Complete AI timeline. *Enterprise AI.* https://www.techtarget.com/searchenterpriseai/tip/The-history-of-artificial-intelligence-Complete-AI-timeline

Karl, T. (2024, June 28). Master AI with Python: Step-by-step learning path. *New Horizons.* https://www.newhorizons.com/resources/blog/learn-ai-with-python

Krebs, B. (2019, April 19). Marcus "MalwareTech" Hutchins pleads guilty to writing, selling banking malware. *Krebs on Security.* https://krebsonsecurity.com/2019/04/marcus-malwaretech-hutchins-pleads-guilty-to-writing-selling-banking-malware/

Kulp, P. (2024, January 24). How this early LLM researcher is taking on ChatGPT with his own search engine. *Tech Brew.* https://www.emergingtechbrew.com/stories/2024/01/24/richard-socher-you-dot-com-search

Kurtianyk, O. (2024, February 23). Intelligent ways entrepreneurs can leverage artificial intelligence. *Forbes.* https://www.forbes.com/councils/forbestechcouncil/2024/02/23/intelligent-ways-entrepreneurs-can-leverage-artificial-intelligence/

Lake, K. (2023, November 15). How to personalize learning using AI. *eLearning Industry.* https://elearningindustry.com/how-to-personalize-learning-using-ai

Laker, B. (2024, March 6). More workers need help to become AI-Literate, LinkedIn study shows. *Forbes.* https://www.forbes.com/sites/benjaminlaker/2024/03/06/linkedin-study-shows-more-workers-need-help-to-become-ai-literate/

Leffer, L. (2024, February 20). "AI anxiety" is on the rise—Here's how to manage it. *Scientific American.* https://www.scientificamerican.com/article/ai-anxiety-is-on-the-rise-heres-how-to-manage-it/

Lee, A. (2023, April 17). L'Oréal's Perso custom lipstick to land at YSL. *WWD.* https://wwd.com/feature/loreal-perso-ysl-custom-lipstick-1234693231/

Liu, C., Zhao, C., Wang, Y., et al. (2023). Machine-learning-based calibration of temperature sensors. *Sensors,* 23(17), 7347. Retrieved from https://www.researchgate.net/publication/373353030_Machine-Learning-Based_Calibration_of_Temperature_Sensors

Lynch, G. (2020, January 16). Smart assistants: A guide for beginners and the confused. *Real Homes.* https://www.realhomes.com/advice/smart-assistants

Madhavan, R. (2019, December 16). Artificial intelligence in policing—Use-cases, ethical concerns, and trends. *Emerj Artificial Intelligence Research*. https://emerj.com/ai-sector-overviews/artificial-intelligence-in-policing/

Marginson, K. (2022, December 8). What products use Z-Wave? *Home Automation Technology*. https://homeautotechs.com/What-products-use-Z-Wave/

Markowsky, G. (2024, July 2). Claude Shannon: Father of information theory, American engineer. *Encyclopedia Britannica*. https://www.britannica.com/biography/Claude-Shannon

Markus, J. (n.d.). Best 20 AI tools in 2024 [Expert Picks]. *Hackr.io*. https://hackr.io/blog/best-ai-tools

Marr, B. (2023, May 12). 15 amazing real-world applications of AI everyone should know about. *Forbes*. https://www.forbes.com/sites/bernardmarr/2023/05/10/15-amazing-real-world-applications-of-ai-everyone-should-know-about/

Marr, B. (2024a, May 7). Spotting AI washing: How companies overhype artificial intelligence. *Bernard Marr*. https://bernardmarr.com/spotting-ai-washing-how-companies-overhype-artificial-intelligence/

Marr, B. (2024b, May 15). Hype or reality: Will AI really take over your job? *Forbes*. https://www.forbes.com/sites/bernardmarr/2024/05/15/hype-or-reality-will-ai-really-take-over-your-job/

Marr, B. (2024, July 29). The essential AI-ready skills everyone needs for tomorrow's jobs. *Forbes*. https://www.forbes.com/sites/bernardmarr/2024/07/29/the-essential-ai-ready-skills-everyone-needs-for-tomorrows-jobs/

Matulionyte, R. (n.d.). A world-first law in Europe is targeting artificial intelligence. Other countries can learn from it. *The Conversation*. https://theconversation.com/a-world-first-law-in-europe-is-targeting-artificial-intelligence-other-countries-can-learn-from-it-236587

McCulloch, W. S., & Pitts, W. (1943). A logical calculus of the ideas immanent in nervous activity. *Bulletin of Mathematical Biophysics*, 5.

McNemar, E. M. (2021, August 13). How to use predictive analytics in chronic disease prevention. *HealthTech Analytics*. https://www.techtarget.com/healthtechanalytics/news/366591042/How-to-Use-Predictive-Analytics-in-Chronic-Disease-Prevention

Merchant, B. (2018, October 1). When an AI Goes Full Jack Kerouac. *The Atlantic*. https://www.theatlantic.com/technology/archive/2018/10/automated-on-the-road/571345/

Michaelzakkovision. (2024, May 22). 15 practical uses of artificial intelligence in daily life. *VISION_FACTORY*. https://www.visionfactory.org/post/15-practical-uses-of-artificial-intelligence-in-daily-life

Milian, J. (2023, September 27). AI in regulation: Applications and use cases. *Ascend Magazine Website*. https://ascend.thentia.com/insight/ai-regulation-applications/

Minvielle, L. (2024, January 24). The 13 best Python libraries for developers in 2024. *We Are Developers*. https://www.wearedevelopers.com/magazine/best-python-libraries

MisterChedda. (2026, June 21). Responsive NPCs: What you wear, drive, and do matters. *Nexus Mods: Cyberpunk 2077*. https://www.nexusmods.com/cyberpunk2077/mods/14800

Moore, P. V. (n.d.). Artificial intelligence in the workplace: What is at stake for workers? *OpenMind.* https://www.bbvaopenmind.com/en/articles/artificial-intelligence-in-workplace-what-is-at-stake-for-workers/

Murphy, R. (2024, October 1). Best budgeting apps of October 2024. *Forbes Advisor.* https://www.forbes.com/advisor/ca/banking/best-budgeting-apps/

Nelson, J. (2024, March 19). Gaming giant Ubisoft showcases how generative AI can upgrade NPCs. *Decrypt.* https://decrypt.co/222460/ubisoft-neo-npc-interactive-voice-chat-gaming

Northumbria University. (n.d.).The 5 Essential Skills For a Job In Artificial Intelligence. *Northumbria University.* https://www.northumbria.ac.uk/study-at-northumbria/courses/msc-computer-science-with-artificial-intelligence-distance-learning-dtdsar6/artificial-intelligence-skills-blog-org/

Obvious. (n.d.). La famille de Belamy. *Obvious AI & Art.* https://obvious-art.com/la-famille-belamy/

Organisation for Economic Co-operation and Development. (2024). Using AI in the workplace. *OECD Artificial Intelligence Papers.* https://doi.org/10.1787/73d417f9-en

Ortiz, S. (2024, February 9). What is Google's Gemini AI tool (formerly Bard)? Everything you need to know. *ZDNET.* https://www.zdnet.com/article/what-is-googles-gemini-ai-tool-formerly-bard-everything-you-need-to-know/

Papadopoulos, J. (2024, June 29). Cyberpunk 2077 just got a must-have mod that enables dynamic NPC reactions; your clothes, driving, and even your past quest choices will now matter. *DSOGaming.* https://www.dsogaming.com/mods/cyberpunk-2077-just-got-a-must-have-mod-that-enables-dynamic-npc-reactions-your-clothes-driving-and-even-your-past-quest-choices-will-now-matter/

Paris, F., & Buchanan, L. (2023, June 17). 35 ways real people are using A.I. right now. *The New York Times.* https://www.nytimes.com/interactive/2023/04/14/upshot/up-ai-uses.html

Patrizio, A. (2024, October 8). 10 top artificial intelligence certifications and courses for 2025. *WhatIs.* https://www.techtarget.com/whatis/feature/10-top-artificial-intelligence-certifications-and-courses

Pazzanese, C. (2020, October 26). Great promise but potential for peril. *Harvard Gazette.* https://news.harvard.edu/gazette/story/2020/10/ethical-concerns-mount-as-ai-takes-bigger-decision-making-role/

Proudfoot, O. (2024, April 15). What is Claude AI, and how does it compare to ChatGPT? *PluralSight.* https://www.pluralsight.com/resources/blog/data/what-is-claude-ai

Programiz. (n.d.). Python strings (with examples). *Programiz.* https://www.programiz.com/python-programming/string

ProjectPro. (2024, April 11). 20 artificial intelligence project ideas for beginners [2024]. *ProjectPro.* https://www.projectpro.io/article/artificial-intelligence-project-ideas/461

Python. (2024, August 7). Welcome to Python.org. *Python.* https://www.python.org/

Python contributors. (n.d.). Signal — Set handlers for asynchronous events. *Python.* https://docs.python.org/3/library/signal.html

Quoatable. (2023, February 3). Barbara Sher quote: You can learn new things at any time in your life if you're willing to be a beginner. *Quoatable.* https://www.

quoatable.com/barbara-sher-quote-you-can-learn-new-things-at-any-time-in-your-life-if-youre-willing-to-be-a-beginner-if-you-actually-learn-to-like-being-a-beginner-the-whole-world-opens-up-to-you/

Sanders, K. (2024, June 25). 17 AI podcasts to listen to in 2024. *The CTO Club*. https://thectoclub.com/best-tools-list/ai-podcast/

Wire, B. (2022, January 13). You may soon change your car's color with the touch of a button. *Dallas News*. https://www.dallasnews.com/business/autos/2022/01/13/you-may-soon-change-your-cars-color-with-the-touch-of-a-button/